CANNABIS INDICA

The Essential Guide to the World's Finest Marijuana Strains

Edited by S. T. Oner

With an introduction
by Mel Thomas

Volume **2**

GREEN CANDY PRESS

Cannabis Indica:

The Essential Guide to the World's Finest Marijuana Strains, Volume 2

Published by Green Candy Press

San Francisco, CA

Copyright © 2013 Green Candy Press

ISBN 978-1-937866-01-3

Dedication

by S.T. Oner

"Mistrust those in whom the urge to punish is strong."
— Friedrich Nietzsche

As always, I wholeheartedly dedicate this book to the fine people at NORML and everyone who has fought for cannabis legalization. It seems to me that success is just around the corner, and with every new State that passes pro medical marijuana laws, our goal comes ever closer. Although there will always be those who seek to punish us for enjoying this plant, I sincerely believe that these people will be in the minority sooner rather than later.

Following the popularity of the first two books in this series, *Cannabis Indica, Vol. 1* and *Cannabis Sativa, Vol. 1*, my thanks go out to everyone involved in this project. I continue to be humbled by the public's support of my books, and I thank you all for allowing me to continue with this adventure. My dream is for someone to read these books in 20 years and recognize the great work produced in our lifetimes.

Thanks go to the fantastic breeders, growers and seed companies who appear here. I wouldn't be able to create a book like this without your incredible support and your brilliant work. This volume features breeders from the USA, Australia, Belgium, Britain, Canada, France, Holland, New Zealand, Russia, South Africa, Spain, Switzerland and others that we can't legally mention.

There are some contributors who wish to remain anonymous, but who deserve recognition and respect nonetheless, as does everyone on the online forums, especially the fine people at Breedbay.co.uk, Meduser.ca, Riotseeds.nl and Seedfinder.eu

Finally, I must thank the growers, breeders and writers who inspired me to learn more about this incredible plant: Danny Danko, Ed Rosenthal, Greg Green, Grubbycup Stash, Jason King, Jeff Mowta, Jorge Cervantes, Matt Mernagh, Mel Thomas, Mel Frank, Nico Escondido and The Rev are some big ones, and of course the unforgettable Jack Herer, may he never be forgotten. I am honored to join you guys in helping to produce memorable works of literature for the global cannabis community. I feel that *Cannabis Indica, Vol. 2* is a valuable addition to the canon of marijuana literature and offers a true glimpse at the genetic potential of the cannabis plant. Were it not for the hard work and sacrifices of the people featured in these pages, a book like this could not exist. For this, I say thank you.

Contents

Preface

Cannabis Indica: An Essential Plant

First of all, I have to say Thank You.

Since my first strain guide, *Cannabis Indica: The Essential Guide to the World's Finest Marijuana Strains, Volume 1* came out in 2011, I have experienced a level of support from the cannabis community that I never could have expected. Not only did so many people read the book that it knocked my socks off, many fans have even written to me personally with letters and emails and through Facebook to express their interest in the guides. I've had people sending me pictures of the first Cannabis Indica book, and my second book in the series, *Cannabis Sativa: The Essential Guide to the World's Finest Marijuana Strains, Volume 1*, poking out of giant bags of bud, being read by their pets and even posing in front of famous monuments all over the world. They've told me how the books helped them choose a suitable medical strain for their particular condition, how they were introduced to new breeders they'd never heard of and how they picked up a copy every time they got high, just to look at the "pot porn" shots within. Every time I hear from a reader, it makes me smile over my morning coffee and bowl of Blueberry Haze, and gives me a buzz greater than the one I get from the weed.

Of course, the breeders also deserve my unconditional respect. From Spain's Dinafem to Australia's Southern Star Seeds, through the USA's Master Thai and Switzerland's Tiki Seedbank, every single seed company found within these pages is doing phenomenal work and helping both medical users and recreational tokers in their respective countries and beyond. The teamwork I see from breeders living in different

Preface

countries and on different continents always astounds me, and furthers my belief that the worldwide cannabis movement is one of the most cohesive and powerful on the planet. With people all over the globe doing such amazing work, we cannot fail to win the war to protect this most sacred of plants.

As ever, in this guide I have tried to represent every corner of the cannabis community. From multinational seed companies to the secret breeder that lives next door, every type of person who dabbles with the genetics of our favorite plant is featured in these pages. I have been so happy to make connections with even more private breeders in the last year, and the effort that these guys and girls put into growing fascinating new plants never ceases to amaze me. At first glance, it may seem as if private breeders and large seed companies are playing different games altogether, but in fact, they are two sides of the same coin. Without the larger companies, we would not have the building blocks that many of the most new and innovative hybrids are created from. Without Sensi Seeds' Afghani #1 plant, we would not have TreeTown Seeds' Purple Afghani, and without Lavender by Soma Seeds, Melon Gum by Spain's Dr. Underground could not exist. By the same maxim, if it were not for the amazing innovations of such breeders as the Joint Doctor and DNA Genetics, the larger companies would have room to rest on their laurels and the breeding game would stagnate. The big companies and the independent breeders exist in a symbiotic relationship, just like humans do with plants: without one, the other cannot exist.

As well as the top companies and independent breeders, I've also had the opportunity to feature genetics and breeders from some new countries. Thanks to the success of *Cannabis Indica, Vol. 1* and *Cannabis Sativa, Vol. 1*, fantastic growers and breeders from such countries as Belgium, Russia and South Africa have sought me

out and expressed interest in being a part of this fantastic grassroots venture. I've also managed to find strains that encompass genetics from every part of the world, and, for the first time, this strain guide features genetics from as far away as Bhutan, Turkey, Lebanon and Laos. Every region has its own interesting and diverse array of cannabis genetics, and it is my honor and privilege to help showcase them to the world. Only in a book like this could you see landrace Lebanese genetics from the Bekaa Valley being preserved and experimented with by a breeder's collective in South Africa. Talk about the global cannabis community!

I'm especially excited to be able to include a very awesome and very elusive American strain in this volume: the enigmatic Zindica from the USA's Bumboklot Seeds. This particular strain was an underground sensation on Overgrow and then disappeared as quickly as it came. It is a beautiful plant with a great smoke, and any cannabis connoisseur has at least heard its name, even if they haven't had the pleasure of tasting its super smooth smoke. I've been able to include even more fantastic North American breeders and their genetics in this volume of the Cannabis Indica series, more in fact than any other strain guide ever created. This is both a testament to the ever-growing North American cannabis scene and the popularity of the first two books, and I hope that this trend can continue!

I'm also thrilled to have the wonderful grower, fantastic raconteur and all round great guy Mel Thomas involved in this project, and am very thankful that he agreed to pen the introduction to this strain guide. Mel's book *Cannabis Cultivation: A Complete Grower's Guide* formed an integral part of my grower's education and I still continue to learn from it now; after all, a man who was named as "a horticultural expert involved in a resolute and successful attempt to grow marijuana on a commercial

Preface

scale" – by the judge who threw him in jail, nonetheless – has a lot to teach us all!

It feels good to be back here exploring the best of indica once again. Indica means many different things to many different people, but to me, indica is like an old friend. While sativa is the excitable, energetic young rascal who drags me to parties that I'm far too old to go to and sends me roaring down a hill on a skateboard that I'm almost certainly going to fly off of at some point, indica is the buddy that I can kick back with at the end of a long and stressful day. Indica is there to calm my nerves when the world kicks my ass and I need to let off some steam. Indica is there to remind me of why *Beavis and Butthead* is so damn funny, and to remind me of my younger days when I was green and stupid enough to do the things I wish I could do now.

For some people, indica is even more important: for them, indica is their pain reliever, the thing that dulls their pain enough to get them to sleep at night. Indica helps their aching bodies get up and out to work, and eases the pain in their arms enough to let them pick up their kids. It brings back the hunger that chemotherapy has robbed them of, and gives their bodies enough energy to fight through to another day.

Many of the strains featured in this book have been used by patients as alternatives to the liver-destroying pharmaceutical medications that had previously ruled their lives. The medicinal benefits of indica strains for conditions that cause chronic pain is undeniable, and I give thanks that an increasing amount of influential doctors are publicly stating this. The number of studies on this subject is also rising, meaning that the pressure on non-smokers and officials to acknowledge cannabis indica's potential medical uses is also increasing. For those who rely on indica strains to manage their medical problems, this is a huge step forward, and should be welcomed by everyone who smokes – medically or recreationally – as it will also help to change the negative

attitudes that consider cannabis to be "a bad thing." While we may all know that cannabis is one of the most natural and most safe medicines available, the general public has been subjected to decades of willful misinformation, and only now is the truth coming out.

We are close to seeing the tide turn in our favor. With more and more reasons to legalize cannabis, it is becoming more and more difficult for politicians to turn a blind eye to the role this plant can play in medicine, therapy, industry and economy. It's sometimes too easy to forget that nations originally formed their governments to look after the people; to create laws and statutes that would adhere to the nation's wants and beliefs, and to keep them safe. George Washington himself said, "The basis of our political system is the right of the people to make and to alter their constitutions of government." Now that Western nations are again realizing the power that the people have, and realizing the rights that have been taken away from them, governments are being forced to realize it, too. When the people rise up and decide to change things, things inevitably change. Because of this, the overwhelming support for the legalization of cannabis will, I'm sure, result in that goal being reached.

In the words of Frederick Douglass, "If there is no struggle, there is no progress."

Keep struggling, my friends.

– S.T. Oner

Introduction

What the Kush? A History of the *Cannabis Indica* Plant
By Mel Thomas

In 1783, a French botanist called Jean-Baptiste Lamarck published the description of a second species of the cannabis plant in his book *Encyclopedia.* Lamarck noted that the species *Cannabis sativa,* normally grown for fiber and textile use, was characterized by a height of 12 to 16 feet, long stalks, sparse foliage, and slender leaves. Cannabis plants native to India, on the other hand, were typically 4 to 5 feet tall at maturity and densely foliated with bushy clusters of comparatively broad leaves; as these plants originated from India, he named them *Cannabis indica L.*

Curious about the origins of the *Cannabis indica* plant I recently decided to spend a few months traveling in India. I had experienced pure *Cannabis sativa* buds in Thailand many years ago and I was interested in finding some pure indica buds at source. India is a strange place with a very diverse culture and they still use *Cannabis indica* in religious ceremonies to this day. Shiva devotees, known as sadhus, can often be seen traveling around the towns and villages smoking charas from clay chillum pipes. India is also a great place to lose weight; I ate a local fish curry and lost 2 lbs. in four days.

My expedition to find the prized *Cannabis indica* buds was a little disappointing to say the least. They traditionally make hand-rubbed charas hashish from their crops and they have no concept of drying and curing the indica buds themselves for consumption. It just seemed like a waste of good buds to me, as the charas varied in quality and even in the north of India I found it was quite harsh to smoke. The hash was very black and slightly pliable, and the herbal cannabis available was not much better. Generally, the bud consisted of seeded flowers that were of poor quality. I soon

Introduction

got the measure of the place and asked a friend who spends a lot of time out there where I could score some good hash. He replied that he would get it for me, explaining, "They like me so they will cheat me less."

I did manage to find some decent indica buds when I visited Goa, but they were from an Austrian guy who grew a small crop every year and paid bribes, known as "baksheesh," to the local police in return for them leaving him alone. I had found myself staying in a small village near a town called Chowdi and it just happened to coincide with the Hindu Holi celebration, which was amazing to watch. During the festivities the Indians throw brightly colored dye at each other and then celebrate in the evening by feasting at each other's houses as all the men of the village go from house to house drumming, chanting and dancing. That evening I sat cross-legged on a floor made from dried cow shit, which passes for concrete in rural India, and, leaning back against a coconut tree, I smoked the pure indica from a clay chillum pipe whilst the sound of drums echoed through the village. It had a strong but indistinct flavor and was certainly a very stoned and chilled experience, but not any different to the strains we now have in the West, which is a testament to the quality of *Cannabis indica* strains available today. All of the excellent plants listed in this edition carry a variation of these indica genes and have a powerful indica stoned effect combined with differing flavors and aromas ranging from pungent skunk to sweet and fruity, depending on the variety.

Although indica is classified as a subspecies of *Cannabis sativa,* recent studies have led researchers to believe that the opposite is probably true and it is now thought that *Cannabis indica* was the first to evolve. More confusingly, many now believe that the sativa vs. indica theory is incorrect, arguing that drug strains of cannabis are: indica, afghanica or kafiristanica, whilst *Cannabis sativa* is primarily grown for fiber. In India, Afghanistan and Pakistan *Cannabis indicas* are traditionally cultivated for the production of hashish, whilst sativas are mainly grown for seeds, fiber or sinsemilla buds, which are not processed into hashish. According to the latest studies, what are now commonly called sativas are actually indicas, whilst what we today call indicas are in fact afghanicas.[1] Modern hybridization has altered the natural development of the cannabis plant as breeders have sought to promote particular traits, blurring the distinction between the two primary species. However, these natural tendencies remain

---

[1] McPartland, J. *The Medicinal Uses of Cannabis and Cannabinoids,* Pharmaceutical Press, 2004: Chapter 4, pp. 74–78.

visible and hybridized plants tend to take on the traits of either indica or sativa strains, depending on which genes are most dominant in the parent plants.

Although *Cannabis indica* refers to Indian-cultivated cannabis, the Afghani indicas were traditionally grown throughout Afghanistan. Whilst many crops were cultivated in the foothills or lowlands, a large number were also grown in the Hindu Kush Mountain regions. This mountain range is between the two countries and Kush weed is thought to be a natural hybrid of afghanica and indica plants caused by airborne pollination. What we now know as *Cannabis indica* originated from these mountainous regions of the Asian subcontinent, which also include Karakoram in northern India, Tibet, Nepal, Bhutan and of course the Hindu Kush mountains in Pakistan and Afghanistan. The Hindu Kush forms part of the Himalayas and the indica plant thrives in this harsh and unforgiving environment comprised of extremely cold winters and hot, dry summers. *Cannabis indica* plants have adapted to this challenging environment by producing short, bushy plants that mature earlier than sativas and interestingly also have more chlorophyll and less accessory pigment to protect the plant from excessive sunlight. As indica strains have more chlorophyll than sativas they grow and mature faster making them well suited for cultivation in temperate climates.

At the highest point in the Himalayas lies the capital of the Chitral District, situated on the western bank of the Chitral River in Pakistan. The town is at the foot of Tirich Mir, the highest peak of the Hindu Kush, and has a dry, almost Mediterranean climate with little rainfall during the very hot summers. The purebred indica strains from this region such as Chitral Kush, the X-18 from Tom Hill and the X-18 Pure Pakistani from Reserva Privada (featured in the first volume of this series) are excellent plants that look similar to Hindu Kush cultivars and have a very characteristic indica leaf shape with a green bluish color that proves their authenticity. These are perhaps some of the best known of the pure Pakistani varieties available today, along with lowland cultivars from the Kashmir Valley such as Vanilla Kush from Barney's Farm, which is an indica-dominant strain whose genetics originate from Kashmir and Afghanistan. There are also other indica-dominant hybrids available such as Mountain Mist, which is a cross between Skunk and a Himalayan Indica.

Not only can indica plants survive the cold, but they are also extremely mold resistant and can withstand heavy nighttime condensation. Purple Kush and other highly regarded strains available today all have Pakistani genetics and many of these old indica strains have been preserved in the United States since the late 1970s, particularly

Introduction

in California. Kafiristanica is said to have evolved from feral indica plants that had escaped from plantations in northern India and in 1929, the Russian botanist Nikolai Vavilov assigned wild or feral populations of *Cannabis indica* in Afghanistan to the group *C. indica Lam. var. kafiristanica Vav.* Both indica and sativa plants can be high in THC; however, cultivated indica strains normally have higher levels of CBD and CBN, whereas wild or feral plants generally display a relatively high CBD content. The higher amount of CBD contained in *Cannabis indica* means that when compared to a sativa, the effects of THC are significantly altered. Whereas *Cannabis sativa* plants are well known for causing a cerebral high, indica varieties have a more sedative effect on the user and indicas are highly recommended for the medicinal properties of their flowers.

Indica strains are extremely effective at treating the symptoms of medical conditions such as anxiety, chronic pain, insomnia, muscle spasms, spasticity in multiple sclerosis, Alzheimer's disease, cancer, HIV/AIDS and tremors caused by Parkinson's syndrome. Indica plants have a higher level of cannabinoids than sativas, which results in a more sedated, relaxed effect on the patient and for this reason many prefer to medicate in the evening. Hybrids of indica and sativa strains can be of enormous benefit to marijuana patients as the resultant plants carry some characteristics from each parent. By adding sativa genetics to indica strains, breeders can produce a plant that has less of a sedative effect on the user and by adding indica to sativa strains, breeders can decrease the sativa tendency to encourage anxiety in some users. Popular strains for medical use include Chronic by Serious Seeds, G-13 Skunk by Mr. Nice Seeds, and Hash Plant by Sensi Seeds.

Indica dominant plants can also be found in northern parts of India, Nepal and Tibet. Other indicas come from the Chinese province of Xinjiang that borders the Himalayas, however, the plants from the southern Chinese provinces of Yunnan and Sichuan are considered to be hybrid varieties of indica and sativa. To the north of Afghanistan are regions that were once part of the former Soviet Union and before that, Turkestan. Cannabis is still traditionally cultivated in these areas, and some of the best indica plants from this region come from Uzbekistan. *Cannabis indica* can also be found in the Middle East and North Africa, particularly Morocco; plants that are more sativa-like in appearance are generally found further south of these areas.

In the United States, during the early 1970s, people were predominately smoking South America sativa smuggled across the border from Mexico. As the War on Drugs intensified, the smuggling of Colombia Gold, Panama Red and Acapulco Gold marijuana

Introduction

into the USA decreased dramatically. Growing these varieties was not successful as the pure sativa varieties did not perform well in the North American climate and it wasn't until the introduction of indica plants from the Hindu Kush regions of Afghanistan and Pakistan that breeders could hybridize the sativas and produce sturdy, shorter plants that were suitable for the North American outdoor growing climate. By breeding pure indica with pure sativa plants U.S. growers were able to reduce the flowering time and produce new hybrid varieties of cannabis strains that are still available today.

Indicas or indica-dominant strains are the indoor marijuana grower's first choice. They produce shorter, stockier plants that mature in less time than sativa varieties and produce heavier yields. Indicas are tough plants that can withstand temperature fluctuations and are very forgiving to the novice grower. Indicas can be grown hydroponically but are also suitable for indoor organic compost grows. However, they prefer a good-size pot to allow their roots to spread out and they should not be overwatered. It is easy to mistake yellowing of the leaves with a nutrient deficiency when in actual fact the roots are drowning in drenched compost. It is advisable to always allow the pot to dry out between watering. Common indica strains for recreational or medicinal use include Kush varieties and Northern Lights. When I grew commercially we favored Northern Lights, which is a pure indica variety that was bred in Holland and is possibly one of the most famous cannabis strains of all time, alongside sativa types such as Haze. This pure indica is ideal for indoor growing; it develops into a hardy, short, stocky plant and it returns heavy yields. After flowering starts Northern Lights plants are mature in around 6 to 8 weeks and once dried and cured it has a very euphoric high. Rather than wait until the plant had completely matured and finished we would harvest when only around 50% of the pistils had turned brown; this seemed to increase the ratio of THC to CBD and made it a more uplifting smoke. *C. indica* is the undisputed heavyweight champion of the cannabis world both in terms of yield and potency, so I hope you enjoy this edition of *Cannabis Indica: The Essential Guide to the World's Finest Marijuana Strains, Volume 2* as much as I did. There are some excellent strains featured throughout the book and they truly represent some of the best genetics that the *Cannabis indica* plant currently has to offer the grower.

CANNABIS
INDICA
The Strains

Afghan Mountain Black

I'm both chonically lazy and vaguely asthmatic, so there are not many things that could get me halfway up an Afghani mountain. This strain, however, might just be one of them. Russian breeders Gibridov.net are the best authority I know on landrace strains from all over the world, and this landrace Afghani is one of a number of strains that they've bred from landrace seeds in their facility, high up in the mountains of Russia!

As a landrace strain this is always going to be less stable and give more expressions than your average grow-lab created seeds. However, Afghan Mountain Black is well worth the extra effort it takes to grow, as this really is a phenomenal plant. Small and bushy, but with great branching and internodal spacing, this looks exactly as in indica should look – and it behaves like it too. These plants enjoy cold weather and can withstand harsh changes in temperature before they feel any effects. They will also be fantastic to make hash from, so make sure you get at least a little!

The high from Afghan Mountain Black, whether smoking the nugs or the fantastic, high-grade has you can make, is absolutely astounding; a pure landrace indica smoke that will put you out of commission for hours unless you're a hardcore toker. This strain is a real treat, and definitely one to look for!

Gibridov.Net, Russia, Pure Indica
Genetics: Landrace Black Mountain Afghani
Potency: THC 14%
gibridov.net

Auto Stoned

In the lead of the auto-flowering game in Spain is Autofem Seeds, who offer a great variety of strains, all with ruderalis in their family tree, making them auto-flowering. The auto-flowering market has experienced a huge surge in the last few years, as these strains are easier to grow, more accessible and as genetically diverse as their harder-to-grow counterparts. Autofem, though, have stayed at the forefront of the breeding pack by bringing more interesting genetics and more stable strains into their repertoire and generally being awesome dudes. Their Auto Stoned strain is a blend of Rosetta Stone and Kush genetics, with the requisite dose of Lowryder from the Joint Doctor to bring the auto-flowering traits in. As anyone familiar with Rosetta Stone, originally from the Brothers Grimm, will know, that strain was celebrated for its high resin production and fast flowering time – two traits that have been well preserved in this Auto Stoned offspring.

If ease of growing is what you're looking for, they don't come much easier than this. As an auto-flowering strain, this plant doesn't need to be subjected to a change of light schedule to flip from the vegetative to the flowering stages; she simply makes the switch when she knows she's ready. She's also a very unfussy plant, growing in soil, hydro and outdoor grows as happily as can be. To get the optimum results from Auto Stoned, the breeders recommend using a hydroponic set up or 12 liters of soil indoors, with 600 watts of light on a cycle of 20 hours on / 4 hours off. Outdoors, you'll be best growing in the south of Europe, and in this region the plants should be finished around May 15th. The rest of Europe will get to enjoy the harvest around the beginning of June. Indoors, the harvest should be around 60 or 65 days from seed, which is a time frame that can allow you 5 to 6 harvests per year – enough to keep anyone knee deep in pot, especially when Auto Stoned gives a yield of 45 grams per plant indoors or 60 grams per plant outdoors.

Autofem Seeds, Spain

Indica-Dominant

Genetics: Lowryder x

(Rosetta Stone x Kush)

autofem.com

When fully finished, cured and dried, Auto Stoned buds are a joy to look at. The biggest pleasure, however, doesn't come from looking at them: the pleasure, of course, is in the smoke. The fruity buds give way to a hashy-tasting smoke that's quite thick and sits nicely in the lungs. The stone, though, is what you are looking for: a nicely balanced head and body high with a slight tendency towards the stone. Your brain will be dancing around nicely inside your head even though your body doesn't want to go anywhere, so sit down and enjoy the feel of the couch for a good few hours!

Berreck

America's M.G.M. Genetics is a passionate medical cooperative that has a magical ability to form fantastic strains as if from nowhere. Of course, they all come from their great breeding stock, which in the case of Berreck is Bubble Berry and Train Wreck. Though the resulting strain sounds like a high class butler in a British period drama, it's far from posh. In fact, it's a rockstar of a plant with great looks and a propensity for fun that's just outside the law!

Due to the heavy sativa presence in this indica-dominant strain, Berreck can take up to 70 days to be fully mature. However, like the gigs of your favorite rock star, Berreck is worth the wait. The plants stay quite short at about 3 feet, but they are also heavy yielders. It will need nutrients in the middle of flowering and will need to be trimmed from the bottom too!

Imagine if you left a fire going near a bowl of overripe fruit in your penthouse hotel suite while you played a gig, then came back to find that your weed had soaked up all that smell; that's exactly what Berreck tastes like. The sweet, woody smell quickly gives way to a fast and racy head high that's got enough body stone in it to slow you down and set you grinning and feeling great for the rest of the week.

M.G.M. Genetics, USA
Indica-Dominant
Genetics: Bubble Berry x Train Wreck
Potency: THC 21%

Black Karma Kush

Karmaceuticals is one of my absolute favorite dispensaries in the U.S. Their dedication to treating patients with both respect and humility gives me renewed faith in the medical marijuana movement every time I hear about them, and the strains that they produce are nothing short of fantastic for those same patients. They're also fun people! This Black Karma Kush was introduced back in 2010, and is a blend of their own Purple Kush and a Karma Diesel plant, which immediately puts

Karmaceuticals, LLC, USA

Indica-Dominant

Genetics: Purple Kush x Karma Diesel

Potency: THC 20.65%

facebook.com/ Karmaceuticals

it up there on my list of Awesome Strains That Have Diesel In Their Lineage!

This is a strain that is happiest growing indoors, and enjoys both hydro and aeroponic set ups. It is a great choice for anyone looking to try a ScrOG grow, as well as those with little space to grow in. With a maximum height of 5 feet and a maximum flowering time of 50 days, this isn't a strain that takes up much in the way of space or time! And, as you can see from the picture, Black Karma Kush buds looks like creatures from another planet! Between their awesome coloration, their growing structure and the foxtailing that they exhibit, I almost want to grow out a whole bunch of Black Karma Kush plants just so I can take glamour shots of them all and hang them up in giant frames around my house – although that might be a little bit weird. No, I'll just have to content myself with having a sneaky peek at those gorgeous buds before smoking them up – although this is a treat in itself! Another treat is the amount of bud you'll have after harvest is over, as each plant averages around 110 grams. That's more than enough reason to invest in some Black Karma Kush!

Karmaceuticals' patients have nicknamed this strain Skittles as it really does taste like the rainbow – and it looks like Skittles too! The very fruity, very sweet taste of this strain makes you feel like a kid all over again, and so does the relaxing, giggly, euphoric high that makes its way into your body and settles in for a good long while. It's not hard to see why Black Karma Kush is so popular in Denver, as it's a fun strain to grow and an even funner one to smoke, with almost no paranoia and a high that makes you giggle like a teenager on the laughing gas!

Blue Angel

No, it's not the name of Beyoncé and Jay-Z's baby, although to be honest Blue Angel would be a slightly less stupid name than the one they gave the poor kid. No, Blue Angel is the name of an even bigger future superstar; a pure indica strain from America's SoHum Seeds. It does, however, share some characteristics with Baby-Z (or is that Beyoncbaby?): not only is it beautiful to look at but its parents are also hella famous! This strain is a cross between a plant that comprised G-13 F1 and Hash Plant

SoHum Seeds, USA

Pure Indica

Genetics: (G-13 F1 x

Hash Plant F1) x

Blueberry

Potency: THC 18%

facebook.com/

SoHumSeeds

sohumseeds.com

F1 genetics, and a Blueberry from the infamous DJ Short. The process of bringing together these three hard hitters took three years, during which all the plants were grown and bred together outside, making this an even more special plant than anyone could imagine.

With an average height of 5 to 6 feet when grown outdoors, this plant is relatively short and can be kept even more so by applying one of a few techniques, such as Low Stress Training and shortening the vegetative cycle if you're growing indoors. Outdoors it can be fantastic in a backyard grow or even a greenhouse set up. The plants grow quickly but with a strong structure and good internodal spacing which allows for lots of bud sites when it enters the flowering stage. You might not need to stake your outdoor Blue Angel plants, but if in doubt, stake them early on as it will be easier than trying to stake them when they're already tall and flowering. It's worth taking good care of these beautiful plants, as each one can yield up to 900 grams of premium pot when grown outdoors. Indoor growers can expect a similar amount per square yard of grow room. Towards the end of the flowering stage the plants' purple hairs will turn browny, and the nugs will be covered in resin; perfect for making hash!

The smoke of Blue Angel is very subtle, but it isn't for beginner tokers; the creative head high and intoxicating effects are best suited to regular smokers or those who are toking for medicinal benefits. This strain is suitable for those seeking relief from chronic pain, nausea, insomnia and loss of appetite along with a whole other list of ailments. A fantastic strain for medicinal and recreational users alike, and one that's as fun to grow as it is to smoke!

Blue Dot

The USA's Green Haven Genetics have got a great little strain here, and one that deserves to make even more of an impact on the U.S. cannabis community as time goes on and more people experience Blue Dot. It's an unknown cross, possibly with some Big Bud and Northern Lights genetics in there, but regardless of its family history it's a strain worth seeking out.

Back in 2000 when it was released, Blue Dot became a firm favorite at dispensaries in Oakland, where the patients loved its medicinal effects. Growers will also love it for its very short stature, good internodal spacing, and its incredibly short flowering time. Blue Dot can be fully ready for the chop in just 6 short weeks, which is great if you're as impatient as me (which I imagine most of you are when it comes to good bud). The best thing about growing this strain is the thick, dense buds that make up your large final harvest – although the high is pretty damn good too!

You'll notice a ChemDawg-like flavor in this smoke, but with generous overtones of Grapefruit and a slight hint of citrus. This complexity also comes through in the smoke, which gives a little head buzz and a huge body stone. This is a fantastic medicinal strain for those dealing with pain or insomnia – and it tastes great too! Now that's the kind of medicine we like.

Green Haven Genetics, USA
Indica-Dominant
Genetics: Unknown, possibly Big Bud x Northern Lights
Potency: THC 18%
greenhavengenetics.com

Blue Magoo

In case you didn't grow up in the US, or have never heard of him, let me tell you a little bit about Mr. Magoo. He's a short, fairly round sort of a man, who doesn't look like anything special but has an amazing ability to come out on top, despite what happens to him. The same could be said of Dynasty Seeds' strain Blue Magoo, expect that this strain is much more attractive than its cartoon character counterpart!

This strain is the offspring of a Blueberry by DJ Short and a William's Wonder F2 plant. Like Mr. Magoo, Blue Magoo is small and squat with quite a bit of weight hanging on its bones. It has a tight bud structure and is pretty greasy, as I've always imagined Mr. Magoo to be too. Unlike the character, this strain is best grown in organic soil and fed organic nutrients, and will need to be staked towards the end of its life to help hold up its fantastically heavy buds!

Blue Magoo is one of those strains that can be great for a million different things, as it adapts to your mood. However, I think the real Mr. Magoo should have smoked some of this plant to help him chill out, as the lavender and berry-flavored smoke of Blue Magoo gives way to a relaxing, narcotic stone that would be great for anyone suffering from stress or anxiety – and he certainly was a bit of a worrier!

Dynasty Seeds, USA
Indica-Dominant
Genetics: Blueberry x MLB (AKA William's Wonder F2)
dynastyseeds.com

Bubba Kush

I've said it before and I'll say it again; if you don't know who Green House Seed Company are, then I don't know where you've been for the last 10 years. I can only assume that either a very extensive coma / a trip to outer space has meant that you haven't been keeping abreast of movements in the cannabis breeding world – and if that's the case, then you've got some big shocks coming your way (Google "autoflowering" and hold on to your hat). Suffice it to say that Green House are the Snoop Dogg of the breeding game, except taller and with more celebrity friends. They're also pretty damn good at making strains that become famous in their own right, and Bubba Kush is one of these. Of course, in North America these days, any strain with Kush heritage is going to be popular, but by using original Kush and the tasty-as-hell strain Bubble Gum Green House have made sure that this strain will be favorite amongst smokers who love with a sickly sweet smoke and a stone that puts them completely out of commission!

As a Kush-derived plant, this strain won't too take too long to flower or get too tall, although it does exhibit a little more sativa influence than some other Kush strains. This means that it can reach 3 or 4 feet in your grow room, and that it will be fully finished in 9 weeks instead of 8. The extra wait is well worth it though; finished Bubba Kush nugs are not only juicy and sweet, but they look like they've been dipped in frosting thanks to all the crystally trichomes! If you like your grow room to look like it's been subject to a very unlikely snowstorm in the last few weeks of flowering, this might the strain for you. Bubba Kush plants grow very quickly and before you know it, they'll be starting school and asking to borrow your car, so be sure to keep an eye on them, especially for signs of mold!

Green House Seed Co., Holland

Indica-Dominant

Genetics: Bubble Gum x Kush

Potency: THC 18.17%

greenhouseseeds.nl

The best way I can describe the onset of a Bubba Kush high is like this: you know when you're somewhere warm, and you decide to cool off my going swimming? You dive into a swimming pool, swim around at the bottom for a little while then come up face first into the warm summer air? Bubba Kush hits you just like that warm air does; it spreads over your face first, then makes it way down your neck and soon it's taken over your whole body, leaving you feel cosy and warm right from the top of your head to the tips of your toes. This wrapped-up-in-a-comforter feeling lasts for hours and hours, meaning that your Bubba Kush stash will go a long way, and also that feel like you're being hugged all evening long.

Canna Sutra

No, its not a well-thumbed book of sexual positions that you can just about wrench your couchlocked body into when you've gone over the top with the Herijuana but are still feeling a little horny – it's a wicked indica strain from Canna Sutra that will, however, put you into the aforementioned frisky state, so make you don't smoke it with your smelly buddy Dan unless you find Dan particularly appealing.

As a blend of a Reclining Buddha mother (which actually sounds quite sexy itself –

or have I been watching that weird porn again?) and a Sensi Star father, Canna Sutra is the flagship strain of Holland's Delta-9 Labs, and for good reason too. It performs better indoors than out, is a big feeder but is sensitive to overwatering, so don't go over the top. This plant finishes in 10 weeks and loves being supercropped!

Canna Sutra is known to elevate your mood, and maybe something else too; if you find yourself "pitching a tent" don't worry, just make sure you've got someone there whose company you enjoy – or you might end up enjoying your own company, more than usual if you get what I'm saying!

Delta 9 Labs, Holland

Indica-Dominant

Genetics: Reclining Buddha x Sensi Star

Potency: THC 20%

delta9labs.com

Caramelice

There are many smokers and growers in Europe and beyond who will tell you that Positronics are there favorite seed company. I am, by nature, indecisive and afraid of commitment, so it would be difficult for me to make such a strong claim, but even I would say that they're definitely in my top five. Consistently bringing out strains that make even the most hardcore cynics sit back and take notice, they're nothing if not exciting. Their Caramelice strain was created by breeding a Hektol plant together with a Redskunk, and, as they themselves say, it is truly a Skunk plant for the 21st century.

Positronics Seeds, Spain

Indica-Dominant

Genetics: Hektol x Redskunk

Potency: THC 16%

positronicseeds.com

This is a hugely vigorous plant right from the get go, with the seedlings shooting up as if the light was a piece of cake and they were a chunky kid. Keep your lights low to minimize the potential stretch, otherwise you'll wake up one day and your week-old seedling will be roughly the size of Kobe Bryant. Your Caramelice plants will have good internodal spacing and will grow small, jagged, light green leaves rather than the fat, deep green indica leaves you might be waiting for. The stems will also stay quite thin, meaning that staking or some other form of support will definitely be necessary before the flowering period. The breeders also suggest constant, heavy ventilation to keep humidity levels moderate, which is a must for Skunk varieties. This ventilation will also help you out a whole bunch when flowering time rolls around and your grow room starts to stink more than a dirty diaper that's been rolled in bear poo and stuffed inside a durian fruit. You should also work to maintain good pH levels and flush with molasses during the last two weeks of flowering; something that experienced growers will have better success with than newbie growers. Caramelice will be finishing in 60 days, and will yield 400 grams per square meter of grow space indoors or the same amount per plant outdoors.

Hints of citrus fruit will be noticeable along with the usual Skunk smell, but it's when you smoke these buds up that the real treat comes in. This fairly balanced high, that's also as smooth as the day is long, will calm the body and get rid of stress as well as increasing your appetite and giving you some nice psychoactive tendencies, making it especially great for a daytime toke!

Cherry Cheese x G-13

Canada's Ganja Creator Genetics is a small and relatively new seed company in the Great White North. Though they're young they're definitely not lacking in ambition, with their own YouTube channel and an ever-growing catalog of fantastic plants. This blend of the famous Cherry Cheese and most talked about marijuana strain in the world, G-13, shows that these guys have enough talent to go far and enough good genetics to get them there!

Cherry Cheese counts Skunk #1 among its parent strains, so be ready for this strain to have a good amount of stink later in the flowering stage. It's a quick grower and has a fantastically high yield, and the good news is that the buds seem to stay fresh forever, so no matter how much or little you smoke, your buds will always taste great.

Cherry Cheese x G-13 gives a high that's heady as well as fluffy in the body, giving you sleepy eyes but keeping your mind bright and awake at the same time. If you can handle a heavy body then this can be a great daytime smoke, but my personal choice is to enjoy this strain when I'm just chillin' at home watching reruns of the X-Files, as it gets me just high enough to get paranoid about it all being true facts and just distracted enough by Gillian Anderson to not worry about it.

Ganja Creator Genetics, Canada
Indica-Dominant
Genetics: Skunk #1 x G-13
Potency: THC 17%
ganjacreator.com

Cherry Hemmingway

Any organic grower who's serious about providing top quality, natural marijuana to themselves or their medical patients already knows about the Rev. As Skunk Magazine's True Living Organics writer, he's the go-to guy for organic weed cultivators who want great advice and beautiful strains. His Kingdom Organic Seeds company produces many organically-grown strains like this one, Cherry Hemmingway, which is a blend of Hawaiian Cherry Bomb, Rez Dog's Firecracker and Bhutan Heirloom genetics. Sounds delicious, no?

This strain is a true hybrid with only a 60% indica influence, so expect it to grow taller than pure indica plants both inside and out. While it can be kept to 3 or 4 feet indoors, outside it explode with 10 feet of growth! Because of this, it is suitable for ScrOG growing as well as natural organic grows, though the latter will bring out the best in this plant. Cherry Hemmy, as its affectionately known, takes 70 days to finish after forced flowering and will yield up to 60 grams per gallon of soil mix used.

Kingdom Organic Seeds by The Rev, USA
Indica-Dominant
Genetics: Hawaiian Cherry Bomb/Rez Dog's Firecracker x Bhutan Heirloom
Potency: THC 19-22%
facebook.com/-
KingdomOrganicSeeds
facebook.com/
TrueLivingOrganics

The Rev warns us that this strain is crazy potent, so newbie tokers should proceed with caution. At higher doses this strain can induce anxiety, so keep it mellow and let your brain basically go numb while your body follows suit. You'll enjoy it, I promise.

Chronic

Ah, Chronic; the strain whose name got hijacked and used indiscriminately by stoners for oh so long. A quick Urban Dictionary search for Chronic will tell you that it's a name for weed with no seeds and just one stem, a name for weed better than White Widow, or a name for weed laced with cocaine. None of them are quite right; it's a three-way Northern Lights, Skunk and AK-47 cross from Serious Seeds that took the marijuana world by storm when it appeared, apparently overnight, on US streets in the mid 90s.

Since the breeders improved this strain in 2000, the medium sized plant has become a real firecracker in the grow room. It only grows to a medium height, but is one of the larger yielding strains, giving up to 600 grams per square meter of grow space both indoors and out. The large central cola will form then surround itself with side branches, making your Chronic crop look absolutely phenomenal. Indoor growers can harvest after 8 or 9 weeks, while outdoor growers should be ready at the end of October, or the start of November at a push.

Serious Seeds, Holland

Indica-Dominant

Genetics: Northern Lights x (Skunk x Northern Lights) x AK-47

Potency: THC 21%

seriousseeds.com

I don't have to tell you how amazing a smoke Chronic is; anything that gets that famous that quickly is bound to be totally out of this world. I will tell you, though, that the balanced high is worth cutting through the bullshit for – so go find some real Chronic!

PHOTOS BY GBI

Colorado Kool-Aid

It's hard to know whether the name of this strain is a reference to its delicious strawberry flavor, or to the fact that anyone who smokes a bowl of Colorado Kool-Aid becomes wholeheartedly devoted to it. I can only assume that the breeders over at Green Life Medical Center have a sense of humor, meaning that it's probably both. It's easy to believe that this strain, which comprises Big Skunk Hawaiian, Black Tie and Great White Shark, could command as much devotion as the People's Temple, though, as not only is the taste fantastic, but the stone is a total body rocker that paints you on to the couch and watches while you dry.

Colorado Kool-Aid plants will only grow to 3 or 4 feet tall, and really enjoy both ScrOG and organic soil grows. It can be grown indoors or out, but the breeders say that this strain absolutely adores natural sunlight. You should water your plants very well, and after harvest, leave the buds to dry in darkness to preserve their vivid pink colorings.

Those lucky smokers in Colorado just love the creeping body stone that this strain brings, as well as huge dose of uncontrollable giggles that accompany the relaxing feeling. Just remember that if you tell people you "smoked the Kool-Aid" they might look and feel more than a little worried – and understandably so!

PHOTOS BY S.C.

Green Life Medical Center, USA
Indica-Dominant
Genetics: (Big Skunk Hawaiian x Black Tie) x Great White Shark
Potency: THC 23%
greenlifemed.com

Cripit

Stoney Girl Gardens, based in the US, are a fantastic collective of breeders and caregivers working to the highest standard possible. Their strains are beyond all others in terms of potency and medical worth, and they have a legion of followers because of this. Cripit, otherwise known as Crippled Pit, was first created in 2008 from a Pit Bull plant and a Cripple Rhino plant, and surprised the breeders by tasting just like Chocolate Thai!

This strain can be grown anywhere, but it grows to 6 feet so be aware of this when choosing your Cripit grow space. Having said this, this is a particularly good strain for beginner growers. Even a small exposure of colder temperatures will turn her deep purple, giving the buds enormous bag appeal! Finishing in only 45 days and giving a yield of around 200 grams, this is a fast one and great if you don't want to wait around for your meds. Keep the temperature in your grow room around 72 degrees Fahrenheit for best results!

Dedicate a long curing time to Cripit, as you don't want to miss out on the equisite flavors of chocolate and sweet candy that will please your taste buds! The high is a very cheerful and "up" one, but also one that gives strong pain relief and help with nausea and insomnia. Stoney Girl Gardens have done it again!

Stoney Girl Gardens, USA

Indica-Dominant

Genetics: Pit Bull x Cripple Rhino

Potency: THC 32%

gro4me.com

stoneygirlgardens.com

Delirium

If you ever had any doubt that World of Seeds are serious potheads, then look no further than the name of this strain. You know that feeling; your head goes all hazy, you can't seem to concentrate on anything in the room, your body feels all tingly and your mind feels nothing short of euphoric even though it's running all over the place not sure what's real and what's not. It's called delirium, and it's what you get when you're absolutely high as hell. World of Seeds have been there just as often as we have, and they love it so much that they've even named a strain after it. This cross between a Mazar-I-Shariff and a Black Domina/Jack Herer plant will most certainly get you into that much-beloved state, and all with a fantastic taste to boot.

The breeders consider this to be one of their best polyhybrids and they spent years developing the strain before they felt comfortable releasing it to the public. Generations of backcrossing have resulted in a very stable strain that expresses insanely uniform crops – in fact, your grow room will look so much like you've bred an army of perfect little plant brothers and sisters that even this might make you feel delirious. The well-known vigor of hybrid plants is well preserved in this plant, and you'll notice your babies growing day by day. Delirium crops are highly resistant to most pests and diseases, although standing water should never be kept in your grow room and you should watch out for signs of white flies all the time. This strain grows par-

World of Seeds, Spain
Indica-Dominant
Genetics: Mazar-i-Sharif x Black Domina/Jack Herer
Potency: THC 15-20%
worldofseeds.eu

ticularly well in a greenhouse grow op, as this will satiate its desire to grow outdoors without allowing it to go back to its landrace roots and grow completely wild! If you do choose to grow outdoors, be sure to keep an eye on your plants and keep them from growing too crazy, and be aware that Delirium enjoys milder climates best. Indoor growers can expect a yield of around 500 grams, while outdoors, this grows to 600 grams after 9 weeks of flowering.

The stinky buds of this plant are potent enough to almost have you feeling high before you've even sparked up a J, but don't be fooled; this is just the start of it! With the heavy, enveloping indica stone that we all know and love, you'll find that your head goes all hazy, you can't seem to concentrate on anything in the room, your body feels all tingly and your mind feels nothing short of euphoric even thought it's running all over the place not sure what's real and what's not. Coincidence? I think not!

Dready Auto Jack

I know that the UK's Dready Seeds just like to name all of their strains with the "dready" company title, but I can't help but thinking of a heavily dreadlocked red-haired Canadian named Jack who likes drinking Pabst Blue Ribbon when I think of this strain. Strangely, that's not actually far from what the finished plant looks like, as its foxtailing buds join up to make dreadlock-like plaits that are covered in little orange hairs. I'm not sure if it likes drinking PBR, though, and I'm not sure I want to test that out.

As a blend of Ruderalis and Jack Herer genetics, Dready Auto Jack is an auto-flowering strain that is particularly easy to grow. As well as not needing any change in light cycle, this strain can adapt very well to almost any type of grow op and fairs especially well in hydro systems. It also grows taller than many other ruderalis-influenced indica strains and can reach up to 4 feet in a hydro set up. The buds will be almost literally dripping with crystals by the end of the 60 days, and each plant will give between 30 and 50 grams of awesome bud.

Dready Seeds, UK.
Indica-Dominant
Genetics: Ruderalis x Jack Herer
Potency: THC 6-12%
dreadyseeds.com

Much like a drunken Canadian, Dready Auto Jack is hella fun; relaxing and energizing all the at same time, pretty chill to hang with all day, and will leave you dazed and confused by the end of the session!

Dutch Delight

Holland's Flying Dutchmen are the breeders that all breeders respect; they've been working in the field for over fifteen years and can always be relied upon to release a strain that makes you get that tingly excited feeling in the pit of your stomach, the one that kids get when they go to bed on Christmas Eve. It's unlikely that I'll ever go to bed one night and wake up to find that some sort of cannabis Santa has filled my worn-through old socks with a few kilos of Dutch Delight, but the thought still gives me the tummy wiggles. This blend of Big Bud, Skunk and Afghani genetics is enough to make any serious toker feel like it's Christmas day, although I spend most of my Christmases feeling gassy and watching old British comedies on the TV rather than getting baked as a ham and looking at my own palms for hours on end. I know which one I'd rather do!

This strain is so indica-dominant that you'll have trouble convincing anyone who sees it growing that it isn't a pure indica. It's a very compact, very bushy little plant that's perfect for bedrooms, attics, dorm rooms and even those stealth grow boxes that are all the rage right now. The breeders bred this plant exactly with these type of grow spaces in mind, as they share my opinion that growing great cannabis should not be restricted to those with a whole spare room to cultivate in! However, the yield and potency of this strain were also key goals for the breeders, and they certainly haven't missed the mark there. After a flowering time that averages 60 days, a 5-foot plant can yield up to 140 grams. That's a huge harvest for indoor plants and can keep the hobby smoker in enough weed to keep him high until New Year's Eve! Dutch Delight plants grown outside can be even heavier yielders, although you should be sure not to expose this strain to too much variable weather as disease can take hold.

Flying Dutchmen, Holland

Indica-Dominant

Genetics: Big Bud x Skunk x Afghani

Potency: THC 17%

flyingdutchmen.com

The smell of Dutch Delight buds will remind you of the best Skunk you've ever had, with that peppery feeling lingering in your nose even while the smoke settles in your lungs. The stone hits much the same as an over friendly and massive English Sheepdog once hit my dad: it will sit on your lap, pin you to the chair and refuse to get off for a good couple of hours. Don't be afraid to just give in and enjoy it, as not even a bowl of the world's best kibble resting on top of Lassie's belly could coax that hound of a stone away from you.

Fayaka

If you ever find yourself hanging around on the streets of Salvador on the north coast of Brazil, you might just be lucky enough to hear a group of people yelling the name of this strain again and again, before launching into some amazing music. Don't worry; this isn't the sign of a marijuana-based uprising in which all gringos will get thrown out of the country so that Brazilians can keep all their amazing pot to themselves. No, this just means that you've come across Public MiniStereo SoundSystem, a dancehall group so popular that Spain's Vulkania Seeds have named this fantastic strain after their well-known war cry. To create this strain, the breeders crossed an '06 cut of New York City Diesel with Nepal Joy, which they believe no longer exists outside of their grow labs. Pretty special, no?

As the landrace indica influence in this plant is so strong, it will stay very small in your grow room. Fayaka plants are like little land mines; hard to spot, but explosive in their results! The plants will be incredibly dense and will pay tribute to their native Nepal by growing incredibly tight little colas that look like small versions of Mount Everest. In fact, if your grow room floor was covered in a thick smog and all you could see was the top of these little mountains, you'd be forgiven for thinking you were tripping into the Studio Ghibli world! Not only are these plants incredibly compact and fantastic in their yield, they also give flowers that are absolutely loaded with trichomes –

Vulkania Seeds, Spain

Indica-Dominant

Genetics: Nepal Joy x New York City Diesel '06

Potency: THC 18%

vulkaniaseeds.com

again, looking as snowy as the top of that most famous of mountains. If you're desperate for a trip to Nepal but can't afford it, invest your money in some Fayaka seeds, a macro lens and a dry ice machine. Before long you'll be posting photos of your grow room on Facebook and nobody will know the difference. To achieve the right effect, keep your plants in the vegetative stage for just 16 days, and allow them between 50 and 60 days of flowering. This will give you a yield of up to 550 grams per square yard of grow room AND an album full of pictures to fool even the most experienced traveler!

Just to complete the whole experience, the effects of Fayaka are much like the effects you would get climbing Mount Everest: light-headedness, body numbness, confusion, drowsiness, and finally, when you reach that peak and look out over the whole gorgeous country, euphoria and a feeling that all is quite well with the world. And it's cheaper than a flight to Kathmandu!

Forfiter Special

Ultimate Seeds have surpassed themselves with this strain, and you don't even have to smoke it to know that it's true. Just look at its family history; if Forfiter Special was to have a Christmas party, ChemDawg DD, Blue Moonshine, AK-47 and New York City Diesel would all be there, surrounded by baby Forfiter Special offspring running into furniture and eating mince pies until they puked. That's quite the family gathering, and one that I, for one, would like to be invited to. With such a background, then, it's clear even on paper that Forfiter Special is an intense mix of indica and sativa genetics, with the indica influence coming out just slightly on top.

The blend of these genetics means that Forfiter Special grows with that well-known hybrid vigor, bursting right out of its seed shells as if seed shells were going out of fashion. Due to the almost balanced indica and sativa influence, these plants will be taller than other indica plants, but not by too much; their size still suits an indoor grow room, as well as an outdoor set up or even a greenhouse grow. Their flowering time is slightly lengthened by the presence of sativa genetics, meaning that they won't be fully finished until 9 weeks have gone by. The slightly airier buds mean that your plants shouldn't be attacked by mold, but it's important to have sufficient ventilation in your grow room just in case. Check your plants daily for signs of pests or problems, as you definitely don't want to end up losing any of these fantastic buds to thrips or white flies! The branching on these plants means that they take especially well to a ScrOG or SOG set up, which will help you to get the maximum yield from however many plants you can have. Pairing this technique with an organic soil grow will ensure that you not only have the biggest harvest of bud, but that you have the best possible tasting Forfiter Special nugs, too. It will be worth it; trust me!

Ultimate Seeds

Indica-Dominant

Genetics: Chemdog DD x Blue Moonshine x AK-47 x NYCD

Potency: THC 19%

ultimateseeds.com

Forfiter Special buds are very sweet smelling, and once you blaze up you'll feel as if you're engulfed in thick cotton candy smoke. These buds are very potent, making them great for medical users, especially ones dealing with more than one condition. If you're dealing with body pain and a more psychological problem, this strain might be great for you. The high is a very balanced one that lingers around for a long, long time and makes even recreational users feel just lovely inside – this is definitely a strain that deserves to be called Special.

Fruit Spirit

Royal Queen Seeds are a great company based in Holland, producing seeds that are nothing less than regal! For this strain, though, I can only assume that they've stopped watching the British royal wedding on repeat and have instead been listening to Nevermind a lot while embracing a healthier diet; this strain smells like Fruit Spirit, and that's because it is! A cross between DJ Short's most fruity of plants, Blueberry, and a White Widow plant, Fruit Spirit buds promise to be as tasty as a gobstopper and as juicy as an especially overripe apple. Could this strain count as one of our five a day? No? Dammit.

Although this plant has a good dose of sativa genetics, it won't grow any taller than 6 feet, even outdoors or in a greenhouse grow. Indoors, it can be kept to 4 feet or smaller, especially with training and techniques such as SOG. If you're growing in the UK or France, you may be limited to an indoor grow with this strain; it does not like the cold one bit, and is much better suited to areas that enjoy a tropical climate and heaps of sunlight, such as Italy or Brazil. In any grow set up, the plant won't stretch much during flowering and instead grows huge main colas that will delight any grower! Fruit Spirit is very resistant to mold and diseases in most climates, though wetter countries can lead to mold in the buds in the later stages of flowering, so be careful to watch for that. The breeders recommend drying the plants for 7 days before harvest, to best preserve the taste and aroma. They suggest a dry trim as the best way to keep your bud tasting amazing. Growers can expect to harvest 40 grams per plant, which translates to 400 grams per square yard of grow space under a 600-watt light. Fruit Spirit plants will take 8 weeks to be properly mature, which means outdoor growers should harvest in early October in the Northern Hemisphere.

Royal Queen Seeds, Holland

Indica-Dominant

Genetics: Blueberry x White Widow

Potency: THC 15-20%

royalqueenseeds.com

Fruit Spirit buds are always going to be as much a treat as a huge ice cream sundae after a healthy dinner, but if you have dry trimmed your buds and given them a long curing period then the flavor of this smoke is going to knock your head right off your shoulders. It's like a mango and a pineapple just had sex in your mouth, and just as you're pondering over how gross that actually is, the nicely balanced head and body high creeps up and slowly takes you over from the inside out. It feels like you might never properly be in control of your head or your body ever again. Oh well, whatever, Nevermind!

Funxta'z Get Rite

Anyone growing organically in the U.S. these days knows about Don't Panic Organix – and if they don't, then they definitely should. California-based breeder Eddie Funxta is becoming a celebrity in the organic cannabis world, with legions of followers already hooked on his fantastic chemical-free strains and growing style. This strain is sure to inspire even more fans, as it's a killer cross between The Who Northern Lights and Eddie's own Funxta'z Triple Platinum OG. The Who Northern Lights is a rare North California indica from the hills of Humboldt County that was gifted to Eddie by a fantastic twenty-five-year veteran grower known only as "S." This was bred with Eddie's favorite Kush to create a stain that would help AIDS and cancer patients needing a strain that was easy to grow and alleviated their symptoms.

Although this strain is technically still in development, it has been making the rounds for five years now, and continues to be improved upon by the breeder. It's happy to be grown either indoors or outdoors, but should always be grown in an organic soil medium without any nasty synthetic additives or nutrients. Be very aware when purchasing your soils and nutrients that labels can be misleading, so make sure it's organic! The growth pattern of Funxta'z Get Rite is very typical of an indica strain, with the well-known Christmas tree-like shape and size when grown outdoors, though it will grow to around 6.5 feet when given enough space. Indoors, the shape is slightly different, with a more flattened canopy and a wider breadth. Be aware of the width of these plants when setting up your grow room, as no one wants to end up with a crop that they can't get through! All this strain needs is 8 weeks to be fully finished, by which time you'll be so keen to get at the buds that you'll almost rip them from the trees. Don't, though. Always harvest with the proper equipment!

Don't Panic Organix, USA
Indica-Dominant
Genetics: The Who Northern Lights x Funxtaz Triple Platinum OG
Potency: THC 18%
dontpanicorganix.com

The name of this strain refers to the fact that when you smoke it, it puts you exactly where you need to be. If you're sleepy or run down, it will either put you to sleep or sit you on your ass and make you chill out (forcibly, if necessary) for as long as you need to. However, if you're bright eyed and bushy tailed, running around like a puppy on steroids, then it will lift you up and let you fly even higher, with a clear, excitable effect and just a little body lethargy. The taste is very diesel-y but with a hint of creamy sweetness too, like eating an organic ice cream while your partner is filling up the car: delicious, but with a background smell of fuel.

G-Bomb

Big Buddha Seeds have long been bringing us the best that the UK cannabis scene has to offer, and they don't look like they're going to let up any time soon. Rather than just working with the same old strains, though, these guys like to improve on the strains that have gone before them, and this offering is no different. The fantastic G-Force, also known just as G, has been kicking around the underground scene in Britain for a while now and has become a fan favorite thanks to its strength and wicked high. Not ones to just rest on their laurels though, Big Buddha Seeds have selected a quality clone of G-Force and have bred it with itself through several generations, to really bring out everything they loved about the original plant. Nice work, guys!

Whether you're as new to growing as a two-minute old child is to breathing, or whether you could put together an aeroponic system blindfolded and using only your teeth, you'll find that G-Force is a fun and easy strain to grow. British breeders have been playing around with it for years and don't seem to be getting bored just yet (although those British are sticklers for tradition). This is a pure indica, and as such, will be short, bushy and incredibly easy to handle both indoors and out. Indoors will be the prime position for G-Bomb, although this resilient plant can take just about anything you care to throw at it – except reruns of that terrible Benny Hill show. It's a medium feeder that enjoys a soil grow as much as a hydro one, so the decision about where and how to grow is totally up to you. You will need to have good ventilation if you grow indoors though, as the nugs on this plant will be so tight and heavy that they practically invite mold in and help it set up its furniture. Ventilation will also be helpful in getting rid of the incredibly pungent smell, although you should be using something like charcoal filters before pushing the Skunk smoke right out of your grow room. Outdoor growers should be ready to chop at the beginning of November, whereas indoor growers can harvest anywhere between 8 and 10 weeks into flowering, depending on how each plant looks.

Big Buddha Seeds, UK
Pure Indica
Genetics: UK G-Force
Clone Only (selfed)
Potency: THC 15%
bigbuddhaseeds.com

The intense spicy smell of the G-Bomb buds might remind you of the awesome curries you had on that drunken night in London, but the flavor is all hash and Skunk. It's the high, however, that has all of the UK loving this strain; the almost-narcotic body stone is very easy to fall in love with, and very easy to fall asleep on, too.

G-13 Skunk (IBL)

Though the infamous Mr. Nice himself hails from the rolling hills of Wales, the seed company that bears his name is based in the country of pot, Holland, and most of their breeding takes place there. Where else could you bring together such classic strains as the governmental myth-laden plant G-13 and an F1 cut of the ever-popular Skunk #1?

With an Afghani ancestry, you would expect this strain not to exhibit much stretch and to be easily manageable in a small space – and it is. It is happy to be grown in both organic and hydroponic systems, although if you're keen to get the best possible taste, organic might be your preferred way to go. It suits a greenhouse set up perfectly, though you should keep an eye on your plants as they can be susceptible to mold. The overall yield can be up to 650 grams per square yard of grow room, when growing in optimum conditions. The flowering time is between 7 and 9 weeks, which translates to harvesting in September in the Northern Hemisphere or late March in the Southern Hemisphere.

Mr. Nice Seeds, Holland
Indica-Dominant
Genetics: G-13 x Skunk #1 F1
Potency: THC 19-21%
mrnice.nl

The taste of G-13 Skunk smoke is slightly fuel-y and slightly peppery, although the main attraction isn't the flavor, it's the effects. Be ready for a beautifully balanced head and body high that leaves no part of you not high!

Grape Diesel

Now, I totally agree with Thomas Jefferson on a lot of things, and the fact that all men are essentially the same is something we can all get along with. However, all Diesel strains are not created equal, and no bill of rights will make this otherwise. Cali Gold Genetics' fabulous Grand Daddy Purple x (Nigerian x Kandahar) hybrid sits high and above its Diesel brethren, in both nobility and effect; and if you don't believe me, get yourself some and try it out!

Expressing two main phenotypes, this strain yields the highest possible amount when given plenty of grow room and a lot of watering. For many people, growing outdoors will be the best way to achieve this, but it can also grow well indoors. This strain is flexible in when it should be harvested, but the breeders recommend somewhere between weeks 9 and 10 for best results. 50% of the plants will grow delicious-looking purple bracts, which combine with the deep green leaves to look like a Monet painting on acid.

Grape Diesel will give you a huge yield of the best quality, so don't be worried about smoking your stash too quickly. The rock hard, berry-smelling buds will explode into a cloud of grape smoke, which will cover you from head to toe and make you melt right into that couch. Now that, my friends, is a Diesel strain.

Cali Gold Genetics, USA
Indica-Dominant
Genetics: Grand Daddy Purple x (Nigerian x Kandahar)
Potency: THC 16.93%
caligoldgenetics.com

Grape Escape

Grape Escape from Canada's Humber Valley Seeds is an enigmatic and exciting strain by a seed company that you're going to be seeing a lot more of in the future. The parent strains may be unknown, but this is definitely an indica-dominant strain with some quality parentage and a whole heap of personality.

As a mainly indica strain you can expect Grape Escape to stay fairly squat and bushy with just a tiny bit of stretch, which can be kept to a minimum by ensuring that the lights are never too far away from the tips of the plants. As with any Grape strain, it can be beneficial to stay with organic soil grows so as not to adulterate the amazing grape taste with any nasty chemical nutrients; even with a molasses flush, the flavor seems to suffer a little. The finished Grape Escape buds will be covered in dank trichomes and, if you're lucky, might have that purple tint that increases the bag appeal by about 1000%.

Aromas of fruit, mint and even licorice come through in this complex and alluring smoke that's best enjoyed from a vaporizer. The subtlety of the taste isn't shared by the stone, though, which is as inconspicuous as a neon elephant in a grey-squirrels-only nightclub and hits with about the same weight. A devastating smoke, for sure!

Humber Valley Seeds, Canada
Indica-Dominant
Potency: THC 19%

Grapefruit Diesel

I've said many times that I'm a fan of all things Diesel – apart from Vin Diesel, who is pretty terrible in all movies except *Pitch Black,* which was fantastically awesome – and this strain just goes to prove even more that Diesel strains really work for me. I've also said that I am a big fan of Canada's Next Generation Seed Company, who primarily work with strains from their home country and the Pacific Northwest, representing North America in the best way possible! This time, Next Gen have taken a luscious Grapefruit plant and bred it into Soma's famous New York City Diesel to create this strain, and in doing so they've caught the fabulous vigor of the hybrid as well as the great taste and killer high of the parent strains, too.

The breeders at Next Generation chose this particular phenotype to stabilize as it was the fastest-flowering Diesel that they had ever come across, and they wanted to hang on to this fantastic trait to make this strain even easier to grow. It's already far from a chore to deal with, as it's got a maximum height of 6 feet and can stay as

Next Generation Seed Company, Canada

Indcia-Dominant

Genetics: Grapefruit x NYC Diesel

Potency: THC 15-20%

greenlifeseeds.com

small as 2 feet indoors, but the shortened flowering time puts this strain ahead of many other Diesel plants in terms of speed. Grapefruit Diesel branches out very well during the vegetative stage, making it a good choice for a SOG set up which will help get the maximum yield. The official flowering period of this strain is 55 days, although some growers prefer to leave it for an additional 10 days to allow the flavor and the aroma to become even more pronounced. Whenever you decide to harvest, you'll get somewhere in the region of 400 grams per square yard of grow room. The finished buds will be so purple that they almost look black, and will be so covered in trichomes that it seems as if diamonds have been pressed into them to "vajazzle" them up! This is a great strain for rookie and intermediate growers alike, so look out for those seeds!

The main draw of any Grapefruit strain will always be the phenomenal taste and smell, but this strain has the added benefit of that telltale oil-and-spice combination of the Diesel family. If you decided to leave your plants for that little bit longer this fantastic combination of sweets will be that more pronounced, but if you chopped early, they'll still be strong enough to render your mouth completely amazed. The high is pure Diesel: heady, then slightly psychedelic, then relaxing, moving down into the body and settling with no paranoia in the mind, too.

Green Shark

Now, I've had my fair share of encounters with sharks before. I'm no marine biologist, but I did spend a bit of time in Australia and I am a fan of surfing. In fact, one Saturday at Manly beach I went down to the shore and got knee deep before the big shark alarm went off and I almost literally pooped my pants and ran back to shore. Despite the crazy set of about 15 hardcore surfers who didn't move, everyone else stayed on shore for 20 minutes while the 3 dusky whalers that were purportedly circling the waters got bored and swam away. I didn't get a good look at them, but I'm pretty sure they weren't green; in fact, I've never seen a green shark in my life before. Maybe there's a different type of shark that swims of the coast of Hero Seeds' native Spain, or perhaps they just named this Black Domina x Great White Shark cross that way because its got a huge bite. Either way, this is a great strain that kicks your ass before you even know what's happening!

With a genetic history that includes Super Skunk, Brazilian, Indian, Northern Lights and Hash Plant, Green Shark comes from a long line of fantastic hybrids. This plant will grow to a medium height but can also be kept to a fairly short height indoors with minimal effort. One surprising thing is that this strain doesn't display as much vigor as you would expect, and might even seem to be slow at the start of the vegetative stage. Don't worry, though, as these plants are just late bloomers (if you'll pardon the pun) and will catch up to the other plants in your grow room before too long. When you flip them into the flowering stage, they'll experience the kind of growth spurt usually felt by teenage boys who find themselves a whole foot taller than all their friends after one crazy week at the age of 14. They are fairly well branched plants with a good, strong structure, and given the right amount of light, can be huge yielders. Outdoor growers should be sure to stake the plants early on to help them hold their own weight just before harvest. The flowering time of this strain sits at around 60 days.

Hero Seeds, Spain

Indica-Dominant

Genetics: Black Domina (Afghan) x Great White Shark

Potency: THC 22-24%

heroseeds.com

Much like the Bullshark and the ever-feared Great White, Green Shark definitely has a strong bite to it and can make you feel like you've just got your legs in a horrific ocean incident if you go a little overboard (don't pardon that pun; it's there on purpose). This Hero seeds offering is for sure a great medical strain and one that will leave you reeling and recovering for a while!

Hash Plant

Ah, Sensi Seeds. Your strains are like the Louis Vuitton bags of the marijuana-growing world; everyone wants one. For a long time now, Sensi have been bringing out totally new strains that blow everyone out of the water, each of which is then taken up by a whole bunch of other seed companies who either use that strain to create even more amazing offspring plants, or who create their own version of the new Sensi classic. Well, they do say that imitation is the sincerest form of flattery!

Sensi created this strain from an original Hash Plant – one of the finest hash-making true Afghani plants brought over from the Hindu Kush - and a Northern Lights plant, who you might say were always meant to be together. Hash Plant is such a favorite at the Sensi breeding facility that you'll find the genetics in many other strains, too, but only in this strain is the Hash Plant really allowed to come into its own. The prevalence of indica genetics in this cross means that Hash Plant is the ultimate strain for heavy tokers growing indoors; if you want to make your own high-grade hash but you've only got that little space under the stairs to grow in, get this strain. It will stay short and squat throughout its life span, bushing out into a more serious-looking plant in the flowering stage. Outdoor growers shouldn't overlook Hash Plant either, though, as it grows particularly well outdoor in sunny climates when it can be put straight into the soil and allowed to flourish. The flowering period of this strain is amazingly short, being just 45 days in some environments, meaning that whether you're growing indoors or out you won't find yourself sitting by the plants begging them to finish; more likely you'll go out for pizza and return to find an army of them stood in your kitchen demanding to be harvested – and when that happens, you better get more pizzas in, as this harvest is going to take a while! In the perfect environment, Hash Plant can be an absolutely huge yielder, so let's hope you've got a space big enough to dry all the bud!

Sensi Seeds, Holland

Indica-Dominant

Genetics: 75% Hash Plant x 25% Northern Lights

Potency: THC 22%

sensiseeds.com

As you might have guessed, your finished Hash Plant buds will look so resinous you'll think you've dropped them in a bucket of oil while you were working on your truck. I've never seen buds quite so greasy in all my life, and even just the finger hash that you can make after harvest is of the highest quality. That's not to say that this strain doesn't pack a punch in a bong, because it most certainly does, but you'd be a fool not to make up a little stash of bubble hash – just a little one!

Heaven

Holland's Rokerij Seeds are almost setting themselves up for a fall with this strain. Naming anything after the supposed place of eternal awesomeness and hangouts with the seraphim is setting some pretty high expectations (if you'll pardon the pun), though of course this Heaven has the distinct advantage that you don't actually have to die to get there. And that's one serious upside. However, being so ballsy in naming this strain also means that it actually MUST be that good, and with parentage that includes Swiss Sativa, Super Skunk and Northern Lights, I'm very inclined to believe that this strain really does transport you to places you've never been before. Add this to the fact that I am a lot more likely to get into this Heaven than the one that counts St. Peter as its bouncer, and you've got yourself a real convert!

It turns out Heaven isn't above the clouds at all; it's about 5 feet off the ground and can be kept even lower if it's indoors, which is going to make a lot of religious paintings seem very wrong! The nugs of this plant will be nice and tight without being so dense you think they might be harboring a black hole somewhere inside. Their slightly more loose structure means that they are a lot less likely to succumb to mold, although good ventilation will always be key. Good ventilation will also help your Heaven plants be even stronger, and you don't want them to struggle holding their tremendous weight when the end of the flowering stage rolls around. If you think this might be an issue, stake early on to avoid the mess of doing it later! For a medium-sized plant, the yield is absolutely huge; up to 700 grams per square yard is an average, and that's a lot of Heaven to handle! Thankfully the flowering time sits at around 80 days, so you won't be waiting around for most of your life to get to Heaven – unlike most people!

Rokerij Seeds, Holland
Indica-Dominant
Genetics: Swiss Sativa x Super Skunk x Northern Lights
Potency: THC 17%
rokerijseeds.com

I always imagined that Heaven would be full of Greek yogurt, skate ramps and attractive naked people, but in fact it's more of a state of mind; a very warm sort of cerebral high that starts at the top of your head and slowly melts down to engulf the rest of your head and finally your body. They were right about one thing though; it is very long lasting, and you do see some white lights. I'm still waiting on the yogurt and skate ramps, but I reckon if I smoke the rest of this bag they'll turn up eventually. It's official: Heaven rocks, and you don't need to wait until you shuffle off this mortal coil to get there!

Hellriser

No, it's not named after the weird British horror movie featuring the pale guy with all that pointy shit in his face — though with a company name like Evil Seeds you'd be forgiven for making the connection with scary movies. No, Hellriser is an old-school Skunk phenotype that was selected back in the early 90s and has since been grown and loved in Evil Seeds' native Spain, which will delight any lovers of true Skunk strains in Europe and beyond!

Though this plant is only marginally indica-dominant, it still sits shorter than most Skunk plants and as such is perfect for indoor growing. It will also go far beyond what many indoor growers have previously experienced, in terms of quality of the finished product and the amount of bud it gives. It enjoys a very short flowering time, taking between 50 and 55 days to be fully finished, and best of all, it is a massive yielder. Indoor growers can expect up to 800 grams of fantastic Hellriser bud per square yard of grow space.

As with all Skunk strains, Hellriser's high is one that is precariously balanced between a killer head high and a devastating body stone. The exact effects of this strain can depend on how you're feeling that day, but you can expect an all-round high that leaves you thinking about it for days afterwards. A great Spanish strain!

Evil Seeds, Spain

Indica-Dominant

Genetics: Old School Skunk

Potency: THC 20%

evilseeds.es

Herijuana Jack 33

I think the appeal of this strain can be explained by something that happened to me not long ago: I was toking along with a friend of mine who smokes a lot of pot but knows next to nothing about it – you know those people, the ones who don't know their Kush from their tush or their Haze from their elbow. Well, I mentioned that I had some Herijuana Jack 33 in my bag and his eyes lit up: "You've got a Herijuana cross? Jesus man, gimme some of that bud!" In crossing Herijuana with their own Jack 33, Ch9 have bred a strain to tantalize even the least informed of pot smokers – and to absolutely delight those in the know!

A fast finisher, this strain will be done in 7-9 weeks, and will give up to 80 grams per plant indoors when given 35 days of vegetative growth. Outdoor growers can expect between 300 and 450 grams, depending on where they're growing. It's not about quantity with this plant though; the high quality, sought-after rock hard buds are solid gold and should be regarded as such!

Ch9 Female Seeds, Europe
Indica-Dominant
Genetics: Motarebel's Herijuana x Jack 33
Potency: THC 18-20%
ch9femaleseeds.com

With a hashy, chemically flavor, this strain has a very distinct smoke that will put you straight on your ass and sit on your shoulders to keep you there. You'll have no doubt that this is a great indica, though you might not be able to talk about it for a while!

Cannabis Indica The Essential Guide to the World's Finest Marijuana Strains, Volume 2

Hindu Kush Auto

Lowlife Seeds might sound like the sort of company that can't be trusted, but in reality, they're great guys who just like to give themselves a pretty badass name. I can see why, though, as they are pretty badass: they're a UK-based breeder's collective who obviously love the most classic and best loved cannabis strains, as they not only breed with some fantastic breeding stock but their strains, like Hindu Kush Auto, are new upgrades of proven plants to make them the best they can be. In order to make this strain autoflowering, Lowlife have bred Lowryder, the father of all autoflowering strains, with both a Hindu Kush plants and a Master Kush plant, just to bring the everyone's favorite Kush influence right to the front of the mix.

This plant is the ultimate plant for a closet grow or a grow room that's otherwise challenged for space, as Hindu Kush Auto plants will only just grow taller than 1 foot – and not by a lot. These plants won't branch out much or get too wide, and they don't require much root space at all – although you should be sure not to stunt the plant growth by making the container sizes too small. The amount of plants you can get per square meter of grow room is huge with an Hindu Kush Auto crop, be but sure not to stack them too closely together or you'll have no space to get around them and check for things like mold in the later stages of flowering. This strain takes 8 weeks to be properly finished, and as with any autoflowering strain, it doesn't need a change in the light cycle to flip into the flowering stage; just watch this plant mature in its own time. The finished buds will be incredibly dense and heavy, just like a good cheesecake, and they'll be coated in a thick layer of resin that's just begging you to make some hash. A whole cheesecake of hash, perhaps?

Lowlife Seeds, UK

Indica-Dominant

Genetics: Hindu Kush x Master Kush x Lowryder

Potency: THC 17%

seedsman.com

As you would expect from a plant that's part indica, part ruderalis, Hindu Kush Auto gives a deeply indica stone that's almost narcotic in its scope. This means that it's a great strain for medical users with chronic pain, insomnia, loss of appetite or any problems with joints and muscles. Any non-medical users should be aware that they will lose all use of their legs and, in cases of extreme dosing, their arms after smoking this strain – so that salsa class is definitely out, and you might have to check if Dominoes will deliver to the window right behind the couch, because you probably won't make it to the door either. I would be lying if I said that I hadn't had a pizza posted through my front door before, slice by slice, after smoking this strain.

Holland's Hope

To me, the name of this strain evokes a sort of post-apocalyptic stoner society (post-apotcalyptic?), in which Europe's whole marijuana supply has been wiped out in a weed war that left no stem standing. Thin, worryingly clear-headed stoners scurry around their pot-barren countries, covered in the kief dust of combat and turning over every stone to try and find that last elusive piece of bud, or one singular seedling that survived the battle. Finally, after months of sobriety in which the possibility of finding something seemed to disappear, a twenty-year-old woman just outside of Amsterdam spots one fat baby leaf sprouting from what used to be someone's backyard. The whole nation bates its breath as their top growers work to get this little indica baby growing; and grow she does. When she reaches 2 feet in height and begins to flower, the country rejoices, and a clever journalist christens the plant with a name that encompasses the feeling of the nation: she is Holland's Hope.

Of course, in reality this pure indica strain was actually brought to Holland in the early 80s, and was acclimatized to that area to become one of the first pure indica outdoor strains the country ever had. They are a lot less likely to make a movie from this story, but that doesn't make it any less fascinating. In breeding this strain to be perfect for the Dutch climate, the growers also made it heavily resistant to mold and to cold weather – a kind of warrior of the plant world, if you will. Though it won't grow beyond 2 feet tall, Holland's Hope is very sturdy and reliable, with a strong structure

Dutch Passion, Holland

Pure Indica

Potency: THC 14.5%

dutch-passion.nl

and a fantastic yield. Thankfully for my imagined nation of Dutch tokers, Holland's Hope finished in a short 8 weeks (although we all know that's the equivalent of a year when you've got nothing to smoke) and outdoors it will finish in the first week of October. The size of its final harvest can vary greatly according to the conditions it's grown in, but at the top of the scale it's not unusual for one well-grown and much-loved plant to give 1000 grams of bud at the end of its cycle. These buds can actually reach 20 inches in length, which is enough to make even the most confident of male stoners feel a little threatened.

This strain will get even the most hardened smokers absolutely wiped; the taste is very sugary and the stone is mega heavy, lasting up to several hours before it allows you to slide effortlessly into sleep. Hang on – easy to grow, reliable, a massive yielder and a huge couch-locker? If it ever comes down to an apocalypse, this strain really might be Holland's – and the world's – only Hope!

ICE

Holland's Female Seeds are phenomenally dedicated to perfecting their strains. This strain not only comprises genetics from the Skunk Special, White Widow, Aurora Indica and Blueberry lines, but it has been backcrossed and cubed for 12 generations, making it an insanely stable plant that gives fantastically uniform crops.

Although ICE is primarily an indoor strain, it can grow outdoors in a Mediterranean climate without any problems, and will be finished in 8 weeks in this kind of environ-

ment. As you would expect from Female Seeds, these plants are very resistant to stress and it's almost impossible to get them to hermie. A top yield of around 750 grams per plant means that ICE is a good choice for commercial grows as well as smaller medical grows, and people who only want to bother with a couple of crops each year.

ICE is a great indica strain, in that it's a full on body stone with a long-lasting life. Lovers of the more sedate type of high will absolutely love this strain. If you're looking for the strain to smoke before you sit down with the Wire box set, then pick up some ICE!

PHOTOS BY MR. WAGS

Female Seeds, Holland
Indica-Dominant
Genetics: Skunk Special x White Widow x Aurora Indica x Blueberry (stabilized for 12 generations)
Potency: THC 18%
femaleseeds.nl

Ice Cream

There isn't a tastier-sounding strain than Paradise Seeds' Ice Cream – unless some-one's created a Bacon and Eggs strain that I don't know about, in which case, I'm going to spend the next month smoking myself to high heaven on that bad boy. In the mean time, I'll continue to treat myself with this enigmatic hybrid from one of Holland's premier seed companies.

Ice Cream expresses numerous phenotypes, each of which grows quicker than a Dutch kid hitting puberty. It's a fantastic choice for a SOG set up, though you'll have to move quickly or one day you'll open the door to your grow room and be caught in the tangle of pot plants like a fly in an especially sticky spider web. An indoor Ice Cream grow can give up to 500 grams per square yard of grow room after 60 days, while out-doors in early October your harvest can give you upwards of 500 grams per plant.

While some phenotypes of Ice Cream are stronger than others, every one of them exhibits the impossibly creamy flavor that gives this strain its name. It's somewhere between vanilla and raspberry ripple, and unlike the real thing, won't make you horribly fat or leave you with melted cream dripping down your fingers. It will leave you feeling balanced, relaxed and quite focused, and you will probably be reaching for more as soon as you finish it.

Paradise Seeds, Holland

Indica-Dominant

Genetics: Unknown

Hybrid

Potency: THC 22%

paradise-seeds.com

Iranian G-13

It's OK; I know you're excited just by seeing the name of this strain. Admit it! I saw your eyes widen when you turned the page! That's a fairly common reaction when any G-13 strain comes around – after all, we all know it as the strain that the government tried to suppress. However, when you factor in the knowledge that this strain not only encompasses a landrace strain straight from Iran but was also formulated by Canada's fantastic Dr. Greenthumb, the excitement levels go through the roof.

This strain promises an even larger yield than the Iranian Autoflower, though of course it will need a change of light schedule to make it flip into flowering unlike its Iranian counterpart. Indoors, it will grow to 2 feet tall if you force it into flowering at a height of 8 inches. A plant of this size will yield up to 600 grams per square yard of grow space. Outdoors, the yields are even higher, with a 5-foot-tall plant giving up to a whopping 1500 grams! Yes, you read that right! It will finish in mid-September, and has good resistance to frost – not that you give a shit: it yields 1500 grams!

Dr. Greenthumb Seeds, Canada
Indica-Dominant
Genetics: G-13 x Iranian Landrace
Potency: THC 22-24%
drgreenthumb.com

Your enormous pile of Iranian G-13 buds will keep you locked to whatever comfortable seating arrangement you have for the whole next year. You'd better arrange for some sort of pizza delivery service as well as liposuction, 'cos you ain't getting off that chair, son!

Irukandji

Inkognyto over at Illuminati Seeds must be a secret marine biologist or some shit like that. I had absolutely no idea what this strain was named after when I first heard of it, and thought it was the sound someone made when they had a cold and sneezed. A quick Google turned into a whole afternoon of reading about the tiny and ridiculously venomous Australian Irukandji Jellyfish – or, rather, reading about the seriously horrible and equally fascinating effects of their sting. Irukandji stings result in Irukandji syndrome, the symptoms of which can range from the generic sickness and nausea to desperate feelings of impending doom and pain that is so extreme that even with the highest possible dose of morphine, it has led some to say they wish they could rip their skin off. Right…

I sincerely hope that the fantastic Inkognyto named this strain not because the high is similar to the organs-on-fire, childbirth-like effects it gives, but because its parent strains are also named after things equally as terrifying; Mamba and Pestilence.

Illuminati Seeds by Inkognyto, USA

Indica-Dominant

Genetics: Mamba x Pestilence

Potency: THC 18-20%

cannazon.net

If there was a Hall of Fame for scary sounding cannabis strains, all three of these would be in there, but thankfully this plant is a lot nicer than it sounds, with genetics of Bubba Kush and ChemDog in there somewhere. This plant can be grown easily in a variety of scenarios, with coco coir, soil and Deep Water Cultures set ups all working well, although the breeder recommends hydro for the best possible results. If you're pushed for space, this can survive even in a Hempy solo cup grow, although it does have a tendency to stretch if its kept too far away from the lights. Supercropping and lollipopping this strain can both work very well, and should both be done just before you flip the plants into flowering. The yield will be huge, with white frosty buds that look almost too good to be true. Don't worry though, they're not a sting-induced hallucination – although the purple platypuses (platypi?) wearing monocles that are crawling up your grow room might be.

No matter how much Irukjandi you smoke, you will not end up thrashing around on a hospital bed, begging someone to kill you – at least not as far as I know. You will, however, find yourself with beads of cold sweat on your forehead and with your muscles shaking a little. It's an extremely potent strain but that's not the only kicker: it also tastes like coffee and chocolate, and the smoke goes down so smooth a bowl feels like a real treat. Just don't get too high and go swimming in Australia!

Jackpot Royale

The USA's AlphaKronik Genetics are, to my mind, one of the better new-school seed companies currently working out of North America. They always seem to work with interesting genetics, and in my line of work it's always a thrill when you come across a hybrid whose parent plants you've never even heard of. I've been aware of Spacequeen, the plant that fathers this strain, for a long while, but I've never before had the joy of smoking a Las Vegas Purple Kush. The breeders at AlphaKronik chose this mother strain as they wanted to create a plant that would taste just like "grape-crème" soda, and when combined with the vanilla from the Spacequeen father, they got just what they wanted!

Jackpot Royale was created in a very organic manner, with the plants allowed to pollinate each other in the open air. This organic mindset is best carried throughout the entire grow period, although you can grow this strain in other set ups if you really want to. The organic method will ensure that you preserve the grape-crème taste

AlphaKronik Genetics, USA

Indica-Dominant

Genetics: Las Vegas Purple Kush x Spacequeen F2

Potency: THC 21%

facebook.com/alphakronik

basilbush.co.uk

that the breeders were striving for, and growing outdoors will help you get the largest possible yield from this plant. In can also be grown indoors, though, with a maximum height of around 4 feet. There is usually a little more stretch, up to 25% more, when the crop is flipped into the flowering period, but if space is an issue for you, you can always keep the vegetative stage a little shorter. Jackpot Royale has very strong branching and root growth, and the breeders recommend letting the soil go dry before watering again. The flowering time of this strain is around 70 days, which translates to the middle of October for outdoor grows. You can expect a medium-high harvest, and the nugs will astound you by looking like golf balls that have been accidentally hit into a water hazard filled with purple sherbet. This strain is particularly good for the ice-water extraction method, if you're that way inclined.

Along with that grape-crème soda taste that the AlphaKronik breeders were so set on creating (and rightly so), Jackpot Royale smells like an Eton Mess; a British dessert consisting of strawberries, meringue and heaps and heaps of thick cream. The smoke is just as delicious, and the stone is very strong. This is also a great strain for those with medical conditions such as insomnia, anxiety, wasting diseases, migraines and chronic pain. It's not often good medicine tastes like an amazing dessert!

Jade Superfrosty

At first I thought that this strain was named after my high school crush and the cold reception she gave me when I told her I was so in love with her that I wanted to push her face into mine, but then I realized that USA's fabulous medical collective Red Star Farms weren't around then so they couldn't have known my lovelife shame. Instead, Jade Superfrosty is a blend of Superfrost OG and a Vanilla Luna plant that's so covered in white trichomes that you'd think someone had left your buds outside on a particularly snowy night.

This is a 90% indica strain, so it is a fantastic choice for indoor growers and it won't grow beyond a couple of feet in height but will bush out nicely to be a great little yielder. Strong stems and a heavy structure mean that it can hold its own weight even at the end of the flowering period, and the fat leaves mean you won't be able to tear your eyes away from it! The plants should be finished in about 9 weeks or even a little less, and your yield will be medium to heavy.

Red Star Farms, USA

Indica-Dominant

Genetics: Superfrost OG x Vanilla Luna

Potency: THC 17%

redstar420.com

The vanilla taste of the parent plant is unmistakable in this strain, as is the sourness of the OG heritage. When the taste of vanilla ice cream finally subsides, you'll notice that the stone is pure indica; all numb body and confused brain – and isn't that just how we like it?

Kandy Kush

With a name like Kandy Kush you almost expect this strain to come all fluffy and pink and wrapped round a stick, which would certainly be a novel way to consume cannabis but it might be a little dry. Thankfully, the name of this plant refers to the way it tastes and smokes rather than the way it is served. Holland's Reserva Privada already have a solid reputation for producing strains that go beyond the pale, and with this cross between OG Kush and Trainwreck they have certainly proved that that reputation is well deserved.

Kandy Kush is an almost perfect hybrid of its two parent plants, in that it preserves the best traits of both of them and makes each one better. In terms of growing, this plant stretches just like a real OG Kush plant but then fills that structure out just like a Trainwreck. It won't be as tall as a true sativa, but it will take up more room than your other indica-dominant plants. The branching of Kandy Kush means that it can work well with a SOG or ScrOG technique, although outdoor growers would be best advised to let it grow as it sees fit – and it will be a gorgeous plant to behold when its allowed to grow in the earth and behave just as it wants to! Kandy Kush, in my opinion, grows best without excessive use of nutrients and stressful training techniques; a good quality soll and some good, natural sunlight at the very best ways to get the most fantastic Kandy Kush you could hope for. The flowering period, too, is a little longer than usual, sitting at around 10 weeks to ensure the plants are properly ready, but when your crops give an average yield of up to 550 grams per square meter of grow space, you can't really complain!

Reserva Privada, Holland
Indica-Dominant
Genetics: OG Kush x
Train Wreck (T4)
Potency: THC 19%
dnagenetics.com

If you haven't had the pleasure of smoking Trainwreck before, I can tell you that it is about the only strain that's guaranteed to settle down a group of drunk 20-somethings. I regularly keep Trainwreck on hand for when my buddies get a little too drunk and rowdy; a quick smoking session around the corner and suddenly they're all as timid as kittens. This great (and useful) effect is kept in tact in Kandy Kush, with the added benefit of the OG kush taste and smell. These buds smell lemony and give an equally delicious smoke, with an immediately-hitting high that is as more-ish as it is strong. It's impossible not to come back from a second round of Kandy Kush, even though just the first toke gets you as high as a kite that's been caught by the wind and now lingers somewhere around the bottom end of the moon. It's a good job it's not served on a stick, or we might never be able to stop!

Kushman's Silverback Grape Ape

The pioneer of his own veganics grow style, Kyle Kushman is known worldwide for his cultivation skills and for amazing genetics like this strain, which is a variation on the Grape Ape plant. Having grown out three different phenotypes of the original plant, Kyle selected his favorite from the set and bred it out with his veganics style to create a 65% indica strain with its amazing flavor nurtured and enhanced!

As a strong indica dominant, this plant is short and stocky and will rarely need staking until the very end of the flowering period, if at all. This strain is a good choice for an outdoor grow, as it is quite resistant to powdery mildew and changes in temperature as long as they're not too extreme. After 60-65 days of flowering they should be ready for the chop, if you can keep your hands off them that long!

PHOTOS BY MG IMAGING

Kyle Kushman, USA
Indica-Dominant
Genetics: Grape Ape
(Kushman's Cut)
Potency: THC 18%
KushmanVeganics.com
budsandrosesla.com

Kushman's veganics style is known for preserving the flavor of buds and keeping away that nasty chemical taste, so it makes sense that Silverback Grape Ape tastes absolutely amazing. The high is just as good, with a balanced effect that tends slightly towards a killer body stone.

Cannabis Indica The Essential Guide to the World's Finest Marijuana Strains, Volume 2

L.A. Ultra x Bubblicious

Their company might only be a few years old, but the breeders over at Spain's Resin Seeds certainly know what they're doing. They've been active in the scene in Europe for some years now, and they know a damn good breeding strain when they see one – or, in this case, two! L.A. Ultra is said to be a mix of L.A. Confidential and MK Ultra, while the Bubblicious is a blend of original Bubblegum and an F1 Lavender male plant that is know for its taste as well as its effects. By breeding these two plants together Resin Seeds have created an insanely tasty strain that punches far above its weight with its killer high!

As both parent plants are indica-dominant, L.A. Ultra x Bubblicious is a plant that leans strongly towards the indica side of things. This means that your crop will be ideal for an indoor grow or a guerilla grow outdoors, as the plants will be short and compact, almost as if they're hiding from the cops or potential pot thieves! Don't think, though, that because they're so inconspicuous they aren't as special as some of the more flashy strains; this plant is one that has bags of personality and is a lot of fun to grow. The bushy plants react well to a whole host of techniques, including LST and topping, although you should figure out which one best suits your grow room and your grow style before you go ahead and start cutting things off. It can be grown both indoors and outdoors and in hydro as well as soil, although to make sure that awesome taste isn't adulterated with chemicals you might choose an organic soil grow. Whether you grow organic or not, it's always a good idea to do an extensive flush before harvest and maybe even use molasses to get rid of any chemically residue. Harvest will be around the 8 week mark with this plant, which translates to the end of September for outdoor growers in the Northern hemisphere. Indoor growers can expect to harvest around 425 grams per square meter of grow space, while outdoor growers will be treated to around 300 grams per plant.

Resin Seeds, Spain
Indica-Dominant
Genetics: L.A. Ultra x Bubblicious
Potency: THC 18%
resinseeds.net

L.A. Ultra and Bubblicious has a double-pronged attack on your senses, so get ready to be conquered by this most hectic of indica-dominant strains! Not only does the candy-sweet flavor of the Bubblicious parent come through really strongly in both the aroma of the buds and the sweetness of the smoke, but the strength, warmth and noticeable longevity of the L.A. Ultra parent means that the high hits you right between the eyes, leaving you reeling for quite some time like Wile E Coyote after he's been hit with his own badly-placed anvil.

Lady Purple

Holland's De Sjamaan Seeds always have my attention, as they have a great track record for producing very interesting strains with even better names. Even their more "usual" strains go far beyond where other seed companies dare to tread, and this, one of their Kush strains, is a testament to their inventiveness. For Lady Purple, an Afghani Hindu Kush plant was crossed with a Purple Kush straight from the U.S., creating a strain that's as easy to grow as it is to smoke, and is as beautiful as it is effective!

Your experience in growing cannabis and your desired results from Lady Purple should dictate whether you grow this strain indoors or outdoors, as it can grow happily in either. Beginner growers, or those looking to have a very simple grow that gives them great results, should cultivate this plant indoors, where it is ridiculously easy to grow and will give a good return on investment of both time and money. Those who have more experience growing weed and are looking for the largest possible harvest will want to grow outdoors, where yields are increased but so is the level of difficulty. Lady Purple prefers moderate climates, and doesn't appreciate harsh changes in temperature. There is a Jamaican sativa in this plant's family tree, so you can expect it to sit a little taller than many other indicas at around 5 feet. This also extends the plant's flowering time to 70 days rather than 60, but this is no problem at all when your finished product is of such high quality. When your plants are done, you'll have no doubt where the name Lady Purple sprang from; this plant is purple all over! The green leaves will display purple striping, but most striking are the flowers, so purple you'd think they'd been dipped in violet paint and glued back onto the plant. At harvest time, which is the first week of October for outdoor growers, you can expect to get around 300 grams per square yard of grow room; and after harvest, you can expect to make some absolutely killer finger hash, as these incredibly resinous buds will have left lots of crystals on your hands!

De Sjamaan Seeds, Holland

Indica-Dominant

Genetics: Afghani/Hindu Kush x US Purple Kush

Potency: THC 17%

sjamaan.com

The finished Lady Purple buds will smell almost like a bonfire in the night air. Sounds crazy, but it's true; the scents of pine and wood mix with a deeper, smoky aroma as well as a slight fruitiness. The effects of this strain are very indica heavy, with a very strong body stone coming on almost straightaway. Couch lock lovers will really appreciate this strain, and will be reaching for the bong again before too long!

Lavender

Lavender, to my mind, is something that old women smell of, and something that people put in those really weird little pillows that you're meant to put in the microwave. Every true stoner, though, will know Lavender as a fantastic Super Skunk x Big Skunk Korean x Afghani Hawaiian cross from Soma Seeds. This strain really encompasses some of the best genetics from across the globe without losing out on great taste, and any fan of purple strains will be a huge fan of Lavender.

Despite being an indica-dominant strain, this plant displays a few traits that are more typical of sativa-heavy hybrids; it takes 9 to 10 weeks to flower and grows quite leggy. Soma himself recommends that, if you are growing in a SOG set up or simply want to keep your plants short, you should shorten the vegetative period to keep Lavender relatively small. Either way, your yield will be medium but the buds will be amazingly purple!

The Afghani heritage of this strain comes through heavily in the smoke, which tastes almost exactly like good hash and gives a tingly body stone that reaches up and touches the brain gently, too. I'd rather have a smoke that smells like hash than an old lady's perfume any day, and I bet this Lavender relaxes you a hell of a lot more than a stupid hot pillow as well.

Soma Seeds, Holland

Indica-Dominant

Genetics: Super Skunk x Big Skunk Korean x Afghani Hawaiian

Potency: THC 19%

somaseeds.eu

Lebanese Bekaa

Lebanon isn't exactly the first place that many of us would think of when we think of killer weed, but this is entirely an oversight on our part, as the Lebanese strains in this guide show. And who better to give us an education in previously overlooked cannabis strains than Weed.co.za, the fantastic South African breeders and growers who've already schooled us in the nuances of strains from their glorious native country?

This strain is a true landrace indica from Lebanon, although unlike many landrace strains, it is quite easy to grow. Cultivators recommend both topping and training to make the grow even simpler. The vegetative stage naturally stays quite short, stunting the growth somewhat, and the flowering stage should be continued until the leaves are practically dead – around the 12-week mark. This may seem a little odd, but it will ensure the most perfect Lebanese Bekaa smoke you could hope for. Though the original breeder who nurtured this fantastic strain has unfortunately passed away, he gave huge credit to the Spanish cannabis community for the successful domestication of this plant, and so should we.

Weed.co.za, South Africa
Pure Indica
Genetics: Landrace Lebanese Indica
Potency: THC 15%
weed.co.za
ganja.co.za

As a landrace indica, Lebanese Bekaa will absolutely freeze both your body and your brain in a warm cuddle; think of it as lovely numbness, because you'll feel lovely but you won't be able to think of much else.

Lebanese Landrace

Spain's Alpine Seeds continue to rise in my estimation – which is no mean feat, considering that they're already pretty high up there! They're known and much revered in the cannabis community for their highly stabilized niche strains, and you can't get much more niche than pure landrace strains from Lebanon. This Middle Eastern country is actually a hotbed of fantastic cannabis genetics and, much like Morocco, the plants that grow there natively are very similar to the plants that grow in the Hindu Kush in Afghanistan and Pakistan. Cannabis grows mainly in the Bekaa plateau in Lebanon, as well as the coastal areas of the country, and this is exactly where this plant will have initially been found. Alpine Seeds proudly preserves this fascinating genetic specimen, and are saving this amazing plant for possible use as breeding stock.

This Lebanese Landrace will surprise you when growing, as it reaches a slightly taller height than many of its Kush counterparts. It won't grow all that much higher, but it can certainly reach 3 or 4 feet and it won't take its time to get there. Shooting up very quickly at the start of the vegetative stage, your crop might leave you a little worried that it will outgrow your grow space, but don't worry; it will even out and stay moderately sized, and grow gorgeous long colas that will have you taking glamour shots of your plants and drooling over them later. Another positive surprise is the very high calyx-to-leaf ratio, which not only makes your plants that little more beautiful but means that, come harvest time, people will be begging to help you harvest. Lebanese Landrace plants are very hardy, and can resist temperature fluctuations as well as extremes of cold or warm, depending on where they're grown. In its native country, cannabis is grown mainly for the production of hash, so if you find yourself with a Lebanese Landrace grow you'd be a damn fool not to have at least a full day of hash-making from your fantastic plants. Even finger hash can be an amazing treat, but if you have the time to make some bubble hash, you won't be disappointed!

Alpine Seeds, Spain
Pure Indica
Genetics: Landrace
Lebanese Indica
Potency: THC 16-17%
alpine-seeds.net

As your Lebanese Landrace plants finish, they'll have hints of brown and red in the buds and will be particularly resinous. They will smell extremely hashy with hints of oil and spice, but the smoke itself will be unexpectedly sweet with a very distinct aroma. Whether you smoke up the buds or treat yourself to some hash, you'll end up with a very balanced and clear high that will have you searching for flights to Beirut and packing your cleanest bong.

Mango

When I was visiting Australia a couple of years ago, chilling out and smoking some great pot in Australia's cannabis capital, Nimbin, I got a little bit too used to eating their amazing fruits. The mangoes that come down from Queensland are pure little rays of sunlight, so juicy and delicious that I could easily eat 5 a day. Upon leaving Aus, I thought that otherworldly mango taste had left my mouth forever – until I first smoked Homegrown Fantaseeds' amazing Mango.

A cross between KC33 and an Afghani indica, Mango is a very strong indica-dominant strain with just enough sativa influence to make it fun. This dose of sativa means that the flowering time is slightly extended to 8 weeks, or early October if you're growing guerilla, and it means that the plants are slightly taller than they might be but still short enough to easily be grown to full term indoors. Be sure not to overwater your crop and always watch out for mold, but otherwise you can just enjoy looking at your beautiful plants until harvest rolls around!

Homegrown Fantaseeds, Holland

Indica-Dominant

Genetics: KC 33 x Afghani

Potency: THC 19%

homegrown-fantaseeds.com

That first bite of Queensland mango comes rushing back to me when I get my first lungful of Mango smoke; the succulent juiciness, the subtle sweetness, and the pure euphoria of such an amazing taste. This strain gets you glued to the couch and high as a kite! Winner!

Master Thai's Green Dragon BX7

The USA's Master Thai is an absolutely fantastic breeder with many years of experiencing influencing his strains. He works with only the best genetics, like the landrace Turkish indica and landrace Afghani indica plants that date back to 1974 and make up Green Dragon BX7.

This highly stable plant enjoys SOG and ScrOG set ups, as well as soil grows treated with coco coir and bat guano, as recommended by the breeder. Growers should keep the feeding light, and enhance the soil with seaweed and worm castings. Best results occur if the plants are left in vegetative mode for slightly longer than normal and are not fed for 15 days before harvest, with a full flush. Plants can give 200 grams indoors or 340 grams outdoors.

Master Thai Seeds, USA
Pure Indica
Genetics: Landrace Turkish Indica x Landrace Afghan Indica
Potency: THC 22-25%
masterthai.com

Master Thai's Green Dragon BX7 is hands down the best medical strain I've ever come across if you're dealing with chronic pain. It's also a killer smoke if you're dealing with nothing but a craving for some absolutely amazing weed that tastes like fruit!

Mau-Mau

Spain's The Blazing Pistileros are a great young seed company who have some seriously fringe genetics with which to create their awesome strains. Mau Mau, which I originally thought was named after the group that orchestrated an uprising in Kenya in 1952 (everyone knows about that, right?), was created from two equally enigmatic strains; Block Head and an F6 version of Killa Queen. It's actually named after the great graffiti artist from London, who loved the strain so much that he designed the seed packaging! Super cool? I think so.

Like Mau-Mau himself, this strain is super chill. Easy to grow, quick and not afraid of giving a good harvest, Mau-Mau is a plant that will suit beginner growers as well as experienced cultivators. It's not sensitive to fertilizers and the breeders recommend using an organic soil grow for the best results. You can easily get 35 grams of premium bud per plant, after 60 days of flowering under a 400 watt HID lamp, which is more than enough for any hobby grower!

The Blazing Pistileros, Spain

Indica-Dominant
Genetics: Block Head x Killa Queen F6
Potency: THC 16.4%
irievibeseeds.com

The finished buds will have turned golden in flowering and so will look like nugs of rock solid gold hanging off your plant! The smoke is smooth and the taste is pleasant, but it's the high that's the real kicker; a real indica body stone with a nice "dancing brain" feeling.

Meen Green Hillbilly

Marijuana Hillbilly is a popular magazine in the U.S., exploring all facets of cannabis culture and the medical marijuana lifestyle. This strain was developed in the Ozark Mountains between Missouri and Arkansas, and named after Meen Green of Swisher Streets – so it's a U.S. strain through and through! Since its release in 1998, Meen Green Hillbilly has been popular in the underground scene, not least because some heritage seeds from the Ozark Mountains form its basis. These seeds were bred into Purple Power and White Widow, to give an indica-dominant variety with some sativa influence and enough of a balanced high to be a useful plant for medical patients.

This strain can be grown pretty much any way, although its 6 to 7 foot stature can render it too tall for some grow rooms. It is, however, a great choice for a ScrOG grow and can flourish best in a soil set up. The breeders tell me that this is an easy plant, so even the most inexperienced of growers can have a pain-free time growing it. However, it is fun enough that experienced cultivators won't get bored, and will react well to the more complex techniques that longtime growers can bring. It is also resistant to almost all pests and problems, making it even easier to care for. The breeders recommend watering twice daily, keeping the soil moist but not too wet in between feedings. They also recommend feeding your Meen Green Hillbilly crop with 1 cup of raw sugar per gallon of water during the flowering period. Do this just once a week, and stop a week before you plan to harvest. After 7 weeks of flowering, your plants will be fully mature and ready for the chop. Your grow room or guerilla outdoor grow will be a veritable cacophony of colors, with purples, greens and oranges fighting with each other for the chance to display themselves all over your plants. Purple usually wins out, but not before green has given it a run for its money! You can expect to harvest 450 grams from each plant; a huge yield!

Marijuana Hillbilly, USA

Indica-Dominant

Genetics: Purple Power x White Widow x Unknown Ozark Heritage Seeds

Potency: THC 18-20%

marijuanahillbilly.com

team31.net

The breeders insist that you give this strain a good curing period, and don't trim before it's totally ready. You'll be rewarded for your obedience with weed that tastes like sour citrus fruit and just a hint of Skunk. Because the strain is such a balanced hybrid, the effects depend totally on you; some will find it a total couch-locker, while others will experience a soaring high that's very cerebral. Either way, this strain is very uplifting and works great at combating pain even in small doses.

Melon Gum

Dr. Underground is a breeder held in high regard in his native Spain, and its because of strains like Melon Gum that people continue to think of him as some sort of breeding genius. It sounds simple – a mix of Soma's Lavender and Bubblegum from Serious Seeds – but even the simplest things in life can be done well or done badly, and this strain has definitely been created by a master of his art.

Flowering in a short 54 days, Melon Gum is like one of those annoying 14 year olds that's about 6 foot tall when everyone else in their class is still shopping in the kid's section; it peaks early. In fact, if grown in an aero or hydro system the breeder recommends not allowing for a vegetative period at all – and even then, after 7 weeks you can expect a yield of about 700 grams per square meter of grow space. Outdoors, you'll get an absolutely amazing 1000 grams per plant, when grown straight in the ground. It's enough to make you run outside covered in camouflage paint to find a guerilla spot right now!

Dr. Underground, Spain

Indica-Dominant

Genetics: Bubblegum x Lavender

Potency: THC 16-18%

drunderground.com

Your resin-coated Melon Gum buds will look good enough to pop right into your mouth, but don't take the "Gum" name too literally. Pack a bowl of this strain and you'll soon feel like a child chewing a piece of melon-flavored candy, and you'll act much the same way.

Mind Body and Soul (MBS)

Maybe it's the beautiful expanses of nature at its best that Australian breeders The Wizards of Oz enjoy in their native land that makes them feel so spiritual, or perhaps they feel that surfing on the east coast makes them feel particularly centred, just as I did when I was carving off the Sunshine Coast. Or, perhaps, it's the quality of their Australian sativa genetics that gets them off their head and makes them feel all squidgy inside and brings out the hippy inside of them. It could be any, but what's important is that their Mind, Body and Soul strain, created by Moonunit and Wally Duck, is a great strain with genetics of Deep Chunk, Zoid Fuel and C99 that gives a spiritually balanced high!

Though this strain mostly grows like an indica, it can experience some stretch in the vegetative stage thanks to the sativa influence. It tends to exhibit some spread, but overall it is easy to grow, as the breeders were aiming for an easy strain with good medicinal qualities. Plants will take around 70 days to mature and to fully fill out the dense, white nugs.

The high of this strain comes on quickly, giving you just enough time to sit back, try to tame your racing mind and eventually realise the best way to bring your Mind, Body and Soul into alignment.

PHOTOS BY SLAYER AND WIZARDS OF OZ

The Wizards of Oz, breeders Moonunit and Wally Duck, Australia
Indica-Dominant
Genetics: Deep Chunk x Zoid Fuel x C99
Potency: THC 20%
icmag.com/ic/forumdisplay.php?f=20

Molokai Frost

I have often spoken of my love of Hawaiian strains, so it should come as no surprise to you that Supreme Beans of the USA have brought out yet another strain that I think is fantastic. Molokai Frost is a landrace Hawaiian strain from the remote Molokai Island that is rumored to be in the family history of such famous strains as Diesel and ChemDawg.

The genetics of this strain were kept secret amongst local growers for over thirty years before being released to the public. In that time, the growers found that Molokai Frost grows best outdoors in an organic soil grow, although a clay medium in buckets also works well. If you are planning to use nutrients, House and Garden by Van De Zwaan is recommended. These plants will grow between 4 and 6 feet outdoors, as they have a lot of sativa influence making them stretch upwards, and they will finish in under 10 weeks.

These nugs are very unique in that they smell like hay. Yep, as in hay that horses eat. They also give a whiff of Diesel and a bit of that Hazy spice, but the smell is mostly fresh. This strain is very narcotic but, thanks to the sativa influence, has enough of a head high to keep you awake and enjoying yourself while the effects last!

PHOTOS BY SOUTHBAY RAY

Supreme Beans, USA
Indica-Dominant
Genetics: Landrace Hawaiian
Potency: THC 16.4%
supremebeans.net

Narkosis

If you have ever been scuba diving then you'll know what narcosis is. That funny feeling when you get to a certain depth and you suddenly feel like someone's given you 28 shots of Jameson and might even have slipped a hefty dose of ketamine into your cereal; you aren't quite sure how you got into the middle of the ocean, you can't figure out whether those are fish or fish people like the lizards in Fear and Loathing in Las Vegas, and you seem to have lost most of the control you previously enjoyed over your limbs. Though this is a sign that things can get very badly very quickly in a dive, everyone kinda enjoys it; in fact, when I was diving in Ko Tao in Thailand, we divers all had shirts with the narcosis logo on it! The clever breeders over at Spain's Blim Burn Seeds must know that everyone loves this feeling, as the effects of their Critical and Somango cross are so similar that I just know this is going to be every diver's new favorite pot strain!

Your Narkosis grow will be as green as the day is long, and very attractive to boot. These medium-sized plants exhibit foxtailing, which is my absolute favorite trait in cannabis plants and makes me want to frame up the trees and stare at them all day. Don't get carried away with their looks and forget to properly look after them, though; although these plants aren't fussy they'll still need a little TLC to bring the best out of them. Outdoors, you will find that these are hardy plants that can take a lot of stress and don't need to be watered too often. Indoors, the plants will be a little more needy but won't require too much effort. You can expect to be harvesting after 60 days of flowering, which translates to around the end of September if you're growing outdoors. The average yield is around 550 grams, and every single bud will look like a work of art!

Blim Burn Seeds, Spain
Indica-Dominant
Genetics: Critical x Somango
Potency: THC 17%
blimburnseeds.com
semillasdemarihuana.net

The Narkosis buds not only smell as delicious as the fresh fruit you get from a Thai market place first thing in the morning, but the effects are the same as that amazing nitrogen narcosis you get on a deep dive. After just a few puffs from a freshly-cleaned bong you'll be back in the South China Sea, 100 feet deep and absolutely blitzed out of your brain. It's a heady feeling, bringing on a bubble of euphoria, but it also takes your arms and legs away from your body for a little while. If you're aching for the feeling of being right down in the deep blue sea but can't afford the flight back to Thailand, get some Narkosis!

Nice Chunk

Australians have a reputation for straight talking, and having been there, I can tell you its true. They say what they mean, and they don't pull any punches – so if the Aussie breeders at Southern Star Seeds tell you that their strain is a Nice Chunk of some killer bud, you know it's the truth! To create this Nice Chunk, these guys have crossed a female Mr. Nice (yes, I know that sounds strange) with a male B-Chunk plant and in the process have made a heavy yielding plant with a great taste too.

As with many Australians, Nice Chunk grows to 6 feet and above and enjoys being outside. Unlike many Australians, it doesn't drink all that much and smells a little hashy. This strain will take 8 weeks to flower, and it can be grown in almost any type of system, although you should bear in mind that it begins as a branchy plant but fills out after 4 weeks of flowering. Indoor growers should harvest 1.2 grams per single watt of light in the grow room, whereas outdoor growers, with good conditions and some luck, should be able to get up to 400 grams from a single plant.

Southern Star Seeds, Australia
Indica-Dominant
Genetics: Mr. Nice (G-13 x Hash Plant) x B-Chunk
Potency: THC 17%
riotseeds.nl

Once finished, your huge stash of gorgeous Nice Chunks will smell like hash, but will burn with an earthy smell and give a really relaxing but still stimulating head and body high, topped off with a cheerful, energetic and delightful stone!

O.Z. Kush

Holland's The Bulldog Seeds are so well established in the Amsterdam scene that it's hard to think of that city without thinking of them. The Bulldog was one of the first coffeeshops to open before the 'Dam was the tokers paradise we all know and love, and it's still there to this day. The owners teamed up with some of the world's best breeders to come out with a line of their own Bulldog strains, each one with the quality you'd expect from such a well-respected brand! This strain, O.Z. Kush, is a version of America's favorite plant that has been given the Bulldog treatment. A fantastic Kush plant was crossed with a particularly intense Silver Haze, that had been much loved by medical users. The result is a fairly balanced hybrid that leans just over towards the indica-dominant side and delights both growers and tokers!

Though this plant can be grown both indoors and out, the breeders recommend an outdoor grow to get the very best out of O.Z. Kush. The crop with have more stretch than some stronger indica crosses, but it still shouldn't get beyond an average of 6 feet, even outdoors. A good idea when growing outside is to stake the plants very early on, to ensure that they grow the way you'd prefer them to and also to provide extra support for the branches all the way through the flowering period, when the buds can cause strain on the structure. The plant is very indica-like in its colorations, and your grow room will look like a real sea of deep green with accents of white, just like the whitewash from miniature breaking waves. After 10 weeks of flowering the plants should be ready for harvest, which will be a doddle thanks to the high calyx-to-leaf ratio. Both outdoor and indoor growers can expect to yield around 600 grams per square meter of grow space, which is enough to impress experienced cultivators as well as newbies!

The Bulldog Seeds, Holland

Indica-Dominant

Genetics: Kush x Silver Haze

Potency: THC 17%

bulldogseeds.nl

Your frostly little green and white O.Z. Kush buds will have that tell tale Kush smell as well as a taste that's super spicy. This is a great choice for almost all medical users as the high hits both head and body, so if you have issues with chronic pain but aren't the kind of smoker who can tolerate a total couchlocker of a smoke, this strain has enough get up and go to keep you up and going while still taking the edge off your pain or the symptoms of your condition. If you're not a medical user, however, you'll love this as a wake n' bake strain that goes pretty perfectly with a coffee and a croissant in the mornings!

Pacific Coast Kush

The USA's OG Genetics are my kind of patriotic. Flying the Star Spangled Banner in your back yard and refusing to go on holiday anywhere other than Florida is all well and good, but if you want to prove that you're a true American to me, you'll play around with some US genetics and create a plant that's more 'merican than a Big Mac and a KFC bucket meal playing football in front of the White House. That's just what OG Genetics have done in bringing together a Phantom OG plant with an L.A. Confidential; they've brought together two of the finest US strains to create the Captain American of marijuana: Pacific Coast Kush.

The bad news is that if you're not in California or Colorado, or you don't have an excuse to go visit a "friend" over that side of the country, then you might struggle to get your hands on some killer Pacific Coast Kush seeds, as they are only really available in that area. The good news is that once you do get your grubby little mitts on them, you'll be in for a fun ride. Whether you decide to grow these plants indoors or outdoors, they're a great little project to have, and exhibit a relatively short flowering period compared to many other indica-dominant hybrids. I've heard it said that a soil grow is absolutely perfect for this strain, but a hydro or even aeroponic system can also give pretty good results. Growing in 1 or even 2 gallon pots would be the best option for most hobby growers. Pacific Coast Kush crops will stay short and compact, while turning deeper and deeper green over time. The dense nugs of these plants can sometimes fall victim to mold, given that they are so weighty and air can struggle to get through them. Keep en eye on your crops for any sign of moldy buds. Also watch out for powdery mildew on your plants, but with proper care and good ventilation, these problems shouldn't arise. Towards the end of flowering you'll notice the pistils turning a deep orange, which should be a sign that the 8 weeks flowering time is drawing to a close and harvest time is now!

OG Genetics, USA

Indica-Dominant

Genetics: Phantom OG x LA Confidential

Potency: THC 18%

oggenetics.com

If you've ever smoked O.G. Kush then you'll find that this strain whisks you right back in time to the first time you smoked up that particular plant, expect with a vague sense of reverse deja-vu; something is just a little different. The difference here is the L.A. Confidential influence that brings in a nice little cerebral tingle and a calmness to the numbing Kush smoke. This is a strain that every true American, and every fan of US genetics, will love as much as pumpkin pie!

Papa's Candy

Spain's Eva Female Seeds are infinitely likeable. Not only are they fun and knowledgeable in person, but their strains are the same: fun to grow, interesting, and delightful to chill with! Papa's Candy is a cross between a White Pakistani plant and a landrace strain from Laos, so this one is destined to be even more interesting than the rest of Eva Female Seeds' catalog – and that's quite a feat!

Although this strain isn't fully stabilized, all phenotypes are very similar in constitution and growing styles with a strong, hardy stem and a robust plant structure. This strength means that the plant can be grown both indoors and outdoors without being ravaged by the elements outside or being weakened by the lack of breeze indoors. Papa's Candy also stays short and squat throughout its whole growth period, so it's great for both indoor grows and balcony grows in the city – although growers with the latter should be sure that you can't see the plants from above. This is also a fantastic strain for those, like me, who have little patience, especially when they see their gorgeous plants growing, as Papa's Candy finishes fully in 6 to 7 weeks indoors. Outdoors, you should expect to harvest around the middle of October, depending on where you are growing. Harvesting earlier than normal, for example, after 45 days, will give you a much more psychedelic high from this strain, so those that enjoy a touch of sativa influence in their indica smoke would be well advised to chop early. Those that like to leave the harvest until later will enjoy buds sticky with resin and bright with orange-red colors.

Eva Female Seeds, Spain

Indica-Dominant

Genetics: Laotian Landrace x White Pakistani

Potency: THC 17-19%

evaseeds.com

If you're a fan of licorice then you'll love this strain, as not only do the buds smell of anise but the smoke tastes of it, too! This flavor also has hints of summer fruits, making the whole thing taste like one of those awesome candies you had all the time when you were a kid but that don't seem to exist now that you're all grown up. Papa's Candy is also a great strain for medical users, as it can help alleviate the symptoms of asthma as well as giving relief from chronic pain, autoimmune diseases and inflammation in the joints. As previously mentioned, you can manipulate your Papa's Candy plants to give you your preferred type of high, depending on when you harvest them. Early harvest will give a very active high that hits the head as well as the body, whereas a later harvest will give a body stone with just a hint of mindfulness. Pick your favorite!

Point of No Return

Mandala Seeds, based in Spain, are clearly partial to smoking in the same way that I am – by that, I mean excessively. We've all been there: you put down the bong after your millionth hit and completely miss the table, smashing your favorite piece of glassware and getting bong water all over the cat – and you can't get up to do anything about it. That, my friends, is the point of no return, and this amazing blend of landrace Afghani and landrace Mexican genetics will take you there again!

With a flowering time of 70 days, this is a medium strain in both length and height, and it gives a fantastically uniform crop with huge cone-shaped buds. The buds are distinctly airy, though, making them resistant to mold more than their denser counterparts. Expect a harvest of 100 grams per plant in a greenhouse or a huge 1000 grams per plant outdoors!

The complete and utter incapacitation that many of us know and love is exactly what you will get from Point of No Return. This strain is a medical-grade medication with a massive indica body stone, and if you're a medical marijuana user you'll find it can help with chronic pain, MS, muscular spasms and sleep disorders. Everyone else will find it helps you accidentally break your favorite bongs and laugh at shitty TV.

Mandala Seeds, Spain
Indica-Dominant
Genetics: Landrace Afghani x Landrace Mexican
Potency: THC 15.5%
mandalaseeds.com

Pollen Chuck

I'm excited to be able to feature some Belgian genetics in this book, as I am a huge fan of their beers and Georges Lemaître – yeah, I bet you have to Google that one! This strain by Core Seeds, which is a three-way cross between Purple Doja, Pee-Wee and a delicious Sour Diesel plant is now being grown out by the awesome dudes at Canada's OGA Seeds, making it available to more North Americans – so thank you, OGA!

The breeders recommend a SOG grow for this particular plant, as it exhibits the Christmas-tree shape that suits that grow style so well. This strain is a light feeder, but it should be topped and trained to get the best out of it. It's also sensitive to changes in pH and should be kept in a medium humidity, as high humidity can bring about mold into the dense buds. Indoors in 2 gallon pots, each plant can yield up to 45 grams of dry bud, which is not too shabby at all for a hobby grower. This plant will be ready for that all-important chop at around 11 weeks of flowering.

Core Seeds, Belgium, grown by OGA Seeds, Canada

Indica-Dominant

Genetics: Purple Doja x PeeWee x Sour Diesel

Potency: THC 19%

ogas.ca

The fruity, oily smell of this strain will give way to a grape taste and a couchlocker of a stone that's even more potent when smoked through a vaporizer. Sit down with a Belgian beer and say thank you to the Belgians – or, as they would say, "Dank uwel!"

Purple Afghani

The USA's TreeTown Seeds are a great collective proudly based in the Bay Area in California. Their Purple Afghani strain was created from one of the most famous strains ever to come out of the Bay: Purple Kush from Trichome Technologies. They got their keen hands on one of the first available Purple Kush clones in 2004 from Oakland's Blue Sky, then bred it with Afghani #1 from Sensi Seeds in order to smooth out the mold problem that often affects Purple Kush…and they succeeded!

This strain improves upon the great work done by Trichome Technologies by increasing the size of the trichomes, making the buds more airy and making this wicked plant even easier to grow. This plant won't grow beyond 3 feet, and about 40% of the plants will be Purple Kush dominant, making them deep purple with a grape taste. Plants will be finished in 53 days and will give 350 grams of bud per square meter of grow space, or 460 grams outdoors.

The silky smooth smoke with heavy aromas of grape and purple candy goes all the way down past your lungs, sets up camp in your legs and glues them right to the couch. Don't expect to get your body back any time soon, as this heavy indica stone is hanging out there for a while and he won't be shifted without a serious fight!

TreeTown Seeds, USA

Indica-Dominant

Genetics: (Trichome Technologies Purple Kush x Sensi Seeds Afghani #1) F1

Potency: THC 12-16%

treetownseeds.com

harborsidehealthcenter.com

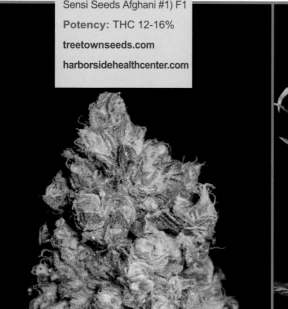

Purple Elegance

Gage Green Genetics are a wicked seed company from the U.S. who are masters at bringing together some of the more fringe strains to create fantastic hybrids, just like this one. Purple Elegance is a blend of Purple Elephant and Joseph OG Kush genetics, the former of which was passed down from the late, great breeder Jo-joRizo (R.I.P.).

Like all the best things in life, Purple Elegance takes a little effort to get. She is not a fan of heat, and prefers environments that are both relatively cool and fairly well controlled, meaning that growing outdoors is out for most people. Don't worry though, because she'll fit right into your grow room without much fuss, and doesn't need too much feeding. Organic nutrients will work best with this strain, as well as pruning. However, you'll need to stake these plants early on as the additional bud sites mean the buds often get too heavy for the branches. Don't worry though – this is great news for your final harvest, which will be nothing short of plentiful!

Gage Green Genetics, USA

Indica-Dominant

Genetics: Purple Elephant x Joseph OG Kush

Potency: THC 17-19%

gagegreen.org

Your Purple Elegance buds will be rock hard and covered in purple stripes, and they'll smell of fuel and grapes. The resulting smoke will set up a fine cloud in your head and refuse to leave for several hours – a bit like a hangover, but a hell of a lot more fun!

Purple Fuck V2

I know what you're thinking; Purple Fuck is what you had on that crazy Wednesday evening a few years back when you went to your friend's art studio, got a little drunk and ended up fumbling in the middle of a pile of paint. Though the memory of that is as persistent as that oil paint was on your pubic hair, this strain isn't referring to that. No, this Purple Fuck is a great strain from everyone's favorite, the USA's Riot Seeds. Along with being the most friendly seed company around, these guys make wicked strains like this one, which is a pretty extensive combination of San Diego Purple Trainwreck, Purple Urkel, Mendocino Purps, Killer Queen and Purple Rhino. The breeders weren't quite happy with the original plant, though it was great in its own right, so this is the updated version of the first Purple Fuck.

The most prized parent strain of Purple Fuck V2 was San Diego Purple Trainwreck, which may or may not still be in existence on its own. Its best traits, though, were preserved in this hybrid, and the plant has been stabilized to express a minimum number of phenotypes. You might never see a more purple plant than this one – even the seeds have stripes of purple in them! Though Purple Fuck V2 can be grown indoors or out, the dense, compact structure makes it perfect for a medical user's indoor grow room or any type of restricted space grow area. The breeder recommends leaving this plant until 8 weeks of flowering have passed, although he did note that a lot of people chop it down at 7 weeks and find that this works perfectly for them. Personally, I prefer the deeper purple color and more intense stone that comes with leaving this strain until a full 8 weeks have gone by, and a good curing process helps to bring out the great purple taste, too.

Riot Seeds, USA

Indica-Dominant

Genetics: San Diego Purple Trainwreck x Purple Urkel x Purple Fuck V1 (Mendocino Purps x Killer Queen x Purple Rhino)

Potency: THC 22%

riotseeds.nl

This strain was created with the intention of bringing forth the antidepressant qualities that the breeder needed most, so those suffering from depression might also find Purple Fuck V2 a great choice for them. Medical users also looking for relief from pain, nausea, Crohn's Disease, IBS or trouble sleeping might also find this strain beneficial to them, whereas recreational users will enjoy the heavy body stone that is lightened slightly by a high that plays around the head a little. It should be noted that this is a very potent strain, and not one that should be smoked by rookie tokers around the back of the college building before going to a party. More experienced smokers and those looking for medicinal benefits will enjoy this strain the most.

Purple Kush x Blue Apollo

The USA's 420Clones are always good for a great strain or two, especially when it comes to providing medical strains that hit the patient's needs. This cross between a Purple version of everyone's favorite, Kush, and a Blue Apollo from Joey Weed is quite like DJ Short's infamous Blueberry, but with more Apollo traits and a subtly different effect.

Sitting at a medium height, these plants exhibit low branching with good internodal spacing and a beautiful uniformity in the crop. It's one of those strains that you can't help taking photos of, especially when flowering finishes and the buds look like purple candy covered in trichomes!

The flavor of this strain is pure Blue Apollo, with almost none of that Kushy dankness lingering around. The high is as clean as the smoke; as transparent as a glass window and therefore great for daytime smoking; they might not even know you're high! High you will be, though, with not a care in the world, as this strain banishes anxiety and leaves you walking on air.

420Clones.com, USA

Indica-Dominant

Genetics: Purple Kush x Blue Apollo

Potency: THC 16-18%

420clones.com

Purple Ryder

Canada's the Joint Doctor has an influence over the cannabis community that continues to spread without him even trying. I bet marketing companies the world over look at the popularity of his Lowryder strain and the myriad strains that have been bred from it, and weep with frustration that they can't come up with a marketing campaign that matches its amazing brand growth potential. Of course, Lowryder's unerring popularity is due to the fact that it literally changed the world of cannabis growing, making it much easier for everyone from hobby growers and medical patients to the best commercial cultivators to grow amazing pot. Without the need for a change of the light cycle, Lowryder transitions into the flowering stage when it's good and ready; a trait known as "auto-flowering." All strains bred from Lowryder also exhibit this trait, meaning that it's big business to breed with Lowryder these days. However, no one does it better than the man himself, and this cross between Lowryder and Mazar is testament to that.

High Bred Seeds by The Joint Doctor, Canada
Auto-Flowering Indica-Dominant
Genetics: Lowryder x Mazar
Potency: THC 12%
jointdoctordirect.com

The result of several generations of a selected hybrid, the very stabilized Purple Ryder will be a favorite amongst closet growers especially, as it stays tiny and compact while still yielding a lot of bud. It's almost impossible to make this bad boy stretch beyond a couple of inches, but just to be sure, keep the lights close to the plants but not close enough to burn the leaves. It's pretty important to do a good flush on this strain if you've used any sort of synthetic nutrients on it, as the flavor of the smoke will be lessened by the nutes and you definitely do not want that to happen here. Even the leaves of Purple Ryder will display a gorgeous range of colors, but this is nothing compared to how your finished buds will look. Weed has never had such bag appeal; if the beautiful Zooey Deschanel was a pot plant, she'd look like this.

It seems strange to describe a flavor as "purple-y," but that's the only way I can describe what Purple Ryder tastes like: purple-y. You know, the way the purple candies taste when you've shoved about 8 of them in your mouth? It tastes that way – and if you smoke enough of it, it will also make you drool as much as a mouth full of candies will. The good news is that you'll get a fairly mild relaxing body stone if you don't overindulge quite that much, although I know that you probably will…and I don't blame you at all.

PHOTO BY DAVID STRANGE

Querkle

If you've ever had the pleasure of meeting the effortlessly hip Subcool, you'll know that not only is his nickname dead on, he's also one of the nicest guys in the breeding business. Along with his Team of Green Avengers, Subcool has become well known for creating very interesting strains from some killer breeding stock. Querkle is a cross between Space Queen and Urkle that's inherited some of the cool of its breeder, making it well worth some attention!

Querkle expresses 2 main phenotypes; one short and grape-like, the other taller and more sativa-influenced. Both these phenos grow faster than the Urkle parent and grow well unstopped in an indoor grow. A ScrOG set up can be a great choice for this strain, but in any set up it will be finished in 8 weeks, with the dense buds sitting heavy on the branches, begging to be harvested!

The smell of Querkle is very grape-like, with hints of other fruit that come through in the smoke as well. The high is very indica, with a fogginess in the head and a heaviness in the body, making it a great all day toke for the serious stoners and a nice night time treat for the more rookie types! Try smoking this out of a clean glass bong for one of the fruitiest tokes you'll ever enjoy, then sit back and enjoy that body buzz we all love!

Subcool and Team Green Avengers, USA
Indica-Dominant
Genetics: Urkle x Space Queen
Potency: THC 14-21%
tgagenetics.com

Cannabis Indica The Essential Guide to the World's Finest Marijuana Strains, Volume 2

134

Rock Star

It probably says a lot about me that when I think "rock star" I don't think of Jon Bon Jovi or Bruce Springsteen, but I immediately think of Steven Tyler from Aerosmith. I mean, come on; the dude has lips that most female American TV anchors would give their right breast implant for, he had an incredibly attractive daughter with Bebe Buell, and he had been around the rehab block 5 or 6 times before I had even been born – and yet he's still going. Sure, he's on American Idol, but I like to overlook that – to me, he's still the Steven Tyler that oozes cool and is totally badass, much like this strain from Holland's Bonguru Seeds. With a Sensi Star parent, this strain already had 'star' genetics right from the offset, and with a Rockbud mother, it couldn't exactly have been a jazz singer. Thankfully for us these two plants came together to create the ultimate Rock Star; a chill, fun plant that gets you mad high!

Like the careers of rock stars the world over, this plant can be a bit of an effort to get started. You don't need to send endless demos out to faceless record companies who are more likely to pour money into the new Lady Beydonna pile of crap than give you a chance, but you do need to pop your beans into some clean water overnight and then plant them straight into small pots, about 5mm down, and water very gently. From these humble beginnings, big things will start; soon your seedling will be bursting out and will quickly become a medium tall plant.

Bonguru Seeds, Holland

Indica-Dominant

Genetics: Sensi Star x Rockbud

Potency: THC 19-20%

bonguruseeds.com

You should vegetative Rock Star until you can see 7 internodes, then flip it into flowering. When it's in its final stage, this plant will start behaving just like Mr. Tyler himself; it will bloom explosively, have no time for pests and become super dense (sorry, Steven!). it will also be in possession of felony-charge levels of resin – just as Steven was when my friend met him around the back of a TV studio in London, tokin' up just before an interview. 70 days after forced flowering you'll be ready to harvest, and manicuring will be a dream! Expect a heavy yield!

They couldn't call this strain Rock Star if it wasn't a crazy high, and this is certainly a stone that won't weigh you down. In fact, quite the opposite; before you know it you'll be tying scarves to your belt, taking your shirt off and running around your room like a madman screaming along to Dude Looks Like A Lady. Don't worry, we've all been there, and this is a perfectly normal reaction to the Steven Tyler of pot strains. Just don't end up judging on American fucking Idol.

Rocklock

After talking to anyone in the Netherlands, you wouldn't think that Holland's DNA Genetics have been around for less than a decade. Everyone has some serious respect for this crew and the strains that they create, as do I, and those Dutch really know their pot so that's some real kudos right there! Indica lovers, however, will have even more reason to love them after they've grown and smoked Rocklock, which counts Warlock from Magus Genetics and Rock Star from Bonguru Beans as its parents.

DNA Genetics, Holland

Indica-Dominant

Genetics: Warlock x Rock Star

Potency: THC 18-21%

dnagenetics.com

With such heavy indica hitters as Mom and Pop, it's inevitable that Rocklock displays all the best traits of that species, bringing much delight to everyone who loves a good couch lock!

As with all good indicas, Rocklock doesn't grow too large at all, making it a fantastic choice for an indoor plant or for an outdoor stealth grow, as it can easily be hidden behind other plants, keeping it away from the eyes of thieves or other "nuisances" (if you know what I mean). It also stays short in terms of flowering time, finishing fully in just 8 short weeks, which is a small amount of time even for an indica-dominant strain. The breeders recommend Rocklock for high-density planting, so use it to make the best out of whatever limited grow space you have; growing shouldn't be limited to those with huge warehouses just begging to be filled with pot, after all! An average yield can be anywhere from 500 to 600 grams per square yard of grow space, meaning that even a spare bedroom can produce enough stellar weed to keep you high for months! The finished buds will be particularly resinous and therefore great for hash-making, although if you do go the hash route be careful – this really is a heavy hitter and even more so when you smoke the hash!

Rocklock is the perfect name for this strain, not just because it brings together both of the parent strains but because it describes almost perfectly what you'll be feeling after a full joint of it – kind of like stoner onomatopoeia, if you will. The heavy smoke will wind its way inside and through your body, making you feel heavier and heavier until you feel that you're made of stone, and it will make your muscles so wiggly that they've got no chance of lifting your rock-solid body from its place on your comfy couch – not that you would want them to!

Royal Purple Kush

There are so many Kush strains around these days that it's hard to keep up. Everyone has their favorite, but I defy any real indica lover not to feel that little tingle of anticipation when they hear the name of a variety they've not tried; I certainly feel that, even now! However, it was so much more than a tingle that I felt when I heard that America's fantastic Emerald Triangle Seeds had a Royal Purple Kush variety. This company should be a favorite of old-school tokers; they specialize in revamping strains from years ago, so I knew that this plant was going to be a special one. The breeders have crossed a Black Afghani with a Bubba Kush to bring the Kush line back to its roots and enhance all that we love about it that little bit more. Good on you, Emerald Triangle!

The vigorous growth of Royal Purple Kush might panic indoor growers at first, as it will seem as if the plant will grow and grow until the top of it breaks through the roof of your grow room. However, you shouldn't worry; this strain only stretches about 20% after you flip it into flower, so you can actually vegetate it for much longer than you can most plants. This growth will, however, give the plants a fantastic structure, and one that's more than ready to burst forth with heavy floral growth in its final stage of life. If purple buds are your thing, or you're looking to add great bag appeal to your final product, the breeders recommend dropping the temperatures in your grow room in the final few weeks, or even (and this is a great little trick) feeding cold water to your plants, making sure that you drop the temperature gradually as to not freak out your whole crop. Outdoor growers in colder climates will enjoy this purple coloring naturally, and should look to harvest around the beginning of October. The flowering time of this strain sits at 9 weeks, and it's a medium-high yielder so be prepared for a busy harvest!

Emerald Triangle Seeds, USA
Indica-Dominant
Genetics: Black Afghani x Bubba Kush
Potency: THC 20%
emeraldtriangleseeds.co.uk

Royal Purple Kush improves upon the already fantastic Kush taste by making it even sweeter, and bringing in the fruity flavor of the Bubba Kush father plant. As if this wasn't enough, that delicious smoke melts into a high that is balanced between both mind and body. Whilst the serenity of a body stone makes its way through your limbs, you'll open your eyes into a very energetic head high that makes you determined, inspired and feeling more than all right. This is a classic contemporary Kush strain for indica lovers everywhere!

Shishkaberry

America's Poor White Farmer Seeds is a lucky man; he has some fantastic contacts in the breeding world, including the kind folks from Eugene, Oregon who gifted him the Shishkaberry seeds that he grew out into this fabulous plant. It was originally created from two Afghani hybrid parents, and shows this indica expression in the way it grows as well as the way it smokes, making it great for medical patients and recreational smokers alike.

Shishkaberry plants have a very low rate of branching but tend to form giant colas that make your grow room look amazing. As the plants get further into the flowering stage the buds will soon turn deep purple and stay that way, giving your finished buds so much bag appeal that modeling agencies will be sniffing around your grow room looking for the talent. You won't have to wait long until you can take the nugs from the plants and set about drying them, but be sure to let them cure for a while to bring out the best of the delicious flavor and aroma.

**Poor White Farmer
Seeds, USA**
Indica-Dominant
Potency: THC 16.1%

It's impossible to mistake the strong blueberry flavor in these buds even when they're still packed inside a baggy. The smoke is like an explosion of fruit in your mouth, which will linger even while the relaxing, pain-controlling narcotic stone sets in – bliss!

Siberian Queen

Ganjah Seeds are a great young company operating out of one of my favorite spots in Spain, San Sebastián. Their Siberian Queen strain is a mix of Skunk and Afghani, and, if she's anything like my friend Afo from Siberia, loves Russian Standard vodka and gives amazing head rubs.

Although you'd assume that, being Siberian, this plant would prefer the bracing cold climate of an outdoor grow in the north, in reality she can be grown indoors as well as out and prefers humid climates. She is pretty strong though, even in the chilly outdoors, and is particularly resistant to disease; it must be all the vodka killing the germs. Indoors, she'll be fully finished in 60 days, whereas outdoors she'll be ready for harvest in the middle of October. Your 2-foot-high plants will be medium to good producers, and will give you deliciously resinous buds that are sparkly enough to hang on a necklace and call jewelry – although that would be a waste of damn good nugs!

The Skunk mother's taste really comes through in the smoke of Siberian Queen, and the balance of indica and sativa makes the high equally balanced; both your body and mind will be full of that enjoyable tingly buzz while your brain runs riot and your body just switches the TV channel over from time to time.

Ganjah Seeds, Spain
Indica-Dominant
Genetics: Skunk x Afghani
Potency: THC 15-18%
ganjahseeds.net

SkaSkunk

Spain's Dr. Canem and Company are a great company and are hands down some of the coolest guys in the breeding world. Every time they bring out a new strain I'm like a kid in a candy store, wanting one of everything and eventually getting so excited that I puke up a little and have to sit down. Their SkaSkunk is a cross between a beautiful Tormento Roja plant and every-popular Skunk #1, and is a nice fuel-smelling plant with a lot of energy!

This plant will grow to a medium height, and might take a little more growing expertise than newbie cultivators possess. However, seasoned growers will have a riot with it, and the gorgeous look of your grow room right before harvest will make the extra effort more than worthwhile. Your favourite nutes will help to plump up the already impressive harvest, but be sure to flush extra carefully to keep that strangely addictive gas flavor strong.

The Skunk #1 parentage doesn't hide away when you smell these nugs, but the high is a nice balance of a Skunk high and a Tormento Roja effect, making it perfect for almost any time or day. The best way to enjoy this strain is to put on some slightly-too-short black pants, pull your white socks up over your ankles, put on Time Bomb by Rancid and dance until your legs no longer have any feeling and you fall straight asleep on your face.

Dr. Canem and Company, Spain
Indica-Dominant
Genetics: Tormento Roja x Skunk #1
Potency: THC 17-19%
facebook.com/drcanem

Skunk NL

Skunk AND Northern Lights? Hell yes! I know you're already sold on this strain without me saying a word, but bear with me here as I am pretty anal about my books and would hate to see the rest of this page totally blank. Canada's Finest Medicinal Seeds is run by the fine team who put out *Treating Yourself,* the medical marijuana journal that is a must-read for all involved with Canada's medical scene as well as those just looking to get some knowledge into them! As such, you would expect their original strains to be focused on giving medical patients exactly what they need, and you would be right. As a cross between Skunk #1 and Northern Lights #5, it comprises two strains that have more than proved themselves over the last couple of decades, and, like Angelina Jolie and Brad Pitt's kids when they grow up, cannot fail to be amazing.

Even though parent strain Northern Lights #5 is known to be a strain that newbie growers sometimes struggle with, Skunk NL is a fantastic choice for beginner growers and medical users who are growing for their own consumption. With a flowering time of 8 weeks and a structure that doesn't get too leggy or too tall, it's a fairy easy ride right through, and it's also a fairly good yielder; outdoor growers can expect to get up to 680 grams per plant outdoors. All growers should be aware that, due to the Skunk #1 influence, this strain is going to stink to high heaven in the later stages of flowering and there's little you can do to stop it. Good ventilation will be key in making sure that the whole rest of your zip code doesn't know what you're doing, and charcoal filters will be an absolute must. Outdoor growers would be advised to plant their guerilla grows far from the prying noses of others, or near a candy floss factory / water filtration plant or some other equally stinky place, so that smell will overpower the smell of the pot!

Finest Medicinal Seeds, Canada

Indica-Dominant

Genetics: Skunk #1 x Northern Lights #5

Potency: THC 16%

finestmedicinalseeds.com

After you've managed to get through the jungle of your grow room and hack down the huge, fairly loose buds at the end of the 8-week period, you will want to give them a good curing period to really get the best taste possible. Your first smoke will make all that effort worthwhile; the smell of freshly made applesauce and ripened fruit gives way to a clean smoke, which in turn slides into a great body stone that also plays around the brain, too. This is a fantastic strain to combat high blood pressure, anxiety, stress and body tension.

Skunkberry

It might sound like a gross name for the little nuggets of poo that those stinkiest of mammals leave behind, but Skunkberry is in fact a strain comprising Pure Skunk and Blueberry F1 genetics to create a Skunk plant that's even tastier than normal. The breeders at Peak Seeds in Canada are known for creating interesting crosses that catch the eye of the community in Canada, and I've a funny feeling that this strain will do exactly that. Even the breeders consider it to be their best plant, which, when you consider the great strains they have in their catalog, is saying a lot!

If you're a beginner grower looking to break into some of the more classic strains without the extra fuss, then Skunkberry might be for you. It's a very easy one to cultivate, with a high tolerance to fertilizers as well as a resistance to any rookie errors you might make. The plants grow large, juicy colas even though they are only a medium height themselves, and they finish in a short 8 to 9 weeks. The harvests from Skunkberry are massive for such a small plant, making them also great for a commercial grower.

Peak Seeds, Canada
Indica-Dominant
Genetics: Pure Skunk x Blueberry F1
Potency: THC 17-19%
peakseedsbc.com

You'll recognize that familiar Skunk smell, but with a good dose of fruitiness in there, too. This is a very fun high that's as mental as it is physical and will leave you ready to party the night away!

Slyder

Sagarmatha Seeds are one of the pillars of the Dutch breeding industry. After almost twenty years in the game they've got a solid reputation that's well deserved, and their original strains have spawned so many imitators and offspring that I wouldn't even be able to count them all. I've always enjoyed their strains that embrace landrace genetics the most, like this one. Slyder is a cross between Northern Lights and an Afghani landrace strain, and was created to harness everything good about the Afghani while taming it so it could be grown indoors. As such, Slyder is a fantastic indica-dominant with a little bit of a wild side!

Indoor growers might feel like Slyder is a gift from the cannabis gods, as it is almost tailor-made for indoor grow rooms and smaller spaces. As well as having a tight, short structure, this plant doesn't smell very much even just before harvest, but it does yield like a plant that's three times its size. Its average height is between 3 and 4 feet, although it can grow a little taller out in the open air, and these plants are so bushy that they almost look like giant fluffy green pinecones. Though this strain will happily grow using almost any technique, the breeders recommend clipping the center cola to ensure that the growth ends up yielding the maximum amount when harvest rolls around. The vegetative period should go on until you can see between 4 and 7 internodes, and then the plant should be flipped into flowering. This period will last between 55 and 60 days before being properly finished, and you'll notice that even into the later stages, you can barely even smell the vast bouquet of dank that resides in your grow room. Once chopped and cured, however, it's a different story altogether; your buds will smell as good as a steak on a BBQ and be even harder to resist! Indoor growers will be stoked to find that after harvest, their yields weigh in at around 300 grams per square yard of grow room; a fantastic result for a plant that is less hassle than a polite great aunt sitting in the corner watching reruns of "Diagnosis Murder."

Sagarmatha Seeds, Holland

Indica-Dominant

Genetics: Afghani Landrace x Northern Lights

Potency: THC 17-19%

highestseeds.com

sagarmatha.nl

Your finished and newly stinky Slyder buds will give off a fairly thick smoke that turns into a very thick stone when it hits your lungs; the strain is named after the I-can't-get-my-feet-off-the-floor gait that smokers walk with after partaking. At even higher doses, this strain will turn even constant tokers into little kittens; or, rather, into polite great aunts sitting in the corner watching reruns of "Diagnosis Murder." Sounds like a great evening to me!

Smile

The UK's Underground Originals crew are masters of marketing. Think of your quintessential stoner – go on, imagine him in your head. What is he doing? He's smiling, possibly with droopy eyes. So what does the name of this strain say to me? It says that it's the ultimate cannabis strain; one that will turn you into the stoner you've always wanted to be, all droopy eyes, confused look but most of all, a Smile. Good work guys.

This indica-dominant plant is as much fun to grow as it is to smoke, and will plaster a grin on your face when you're doing either. This stain stretches very slowly for about 6 weeks after flowering, so you should force flowering when your plants are around half the size that you want them to grow to.

Though Smile grows like an indica, the high is very sativa-influenced and can even be psychoactive if harvested at the right time. There isn't a hint of couchlock, just a bit of a body buzz, but most of the action goes on above your neck, from the fuzzy brain feelings to a grin that wouldn't look out of place on Jack Nicholson's Joker himself.

Underground Originals, UK

Indica-Dominant

Potency: THC 18-20%

ugorg.com

Snow White

Holland's Spliff Seeds have absolutely made my day with this strain. I'm not only stoked that it's named after one of my favorite childhood movies (although the real favorite was Flight Of The Navigator), but they've actually done a little of Disney backstory with this one. The fantastic Spliff Seeds breeders have bred this plant from 3 distinct varieties: Northern Lights, White Widow, and, you've guessed it, Cinderella 99. Of course, Cinderella didn't come out until 17 years after Snow White and the Seven Dwarfs, but let's leave my Disney nerdism aside and just say that this is a wicked hybrid that's super strong!

Indoor growers should make sure that their light distribution is even, otherwise they might end up with one giant plant right under the center of the light and 7 dwarves around the edge. To remedy this situation, move your larger plants to the edge of the lights in the vegetative stage and let the smaller ones catch up! As an 80% indica strain this is never going to get too tall, but it does grow quickly in the vegetative phase. Snow

Spliff Seeds, Holland

Indica-Dominant

Genetics: Northern Lights x White Widow x Cinderella 99

Potency: THC 20-22%

spliffseeds.nl

White is comfortable being both indoors and outdoors, but to make her really Happy grow her in a hydro SOG system and don't let her linger too long in the vegetative stage, or she'll get a little Sleepy – 3 weeks is usually good. Unfortunately, if she's riddled with disease she won't alert you by being Sneezy, so you'll have to keep an eye out for mold and powdery mildew instead. Hopefully you won't need to call the Doc. Overwatering will make her pretty Grumpy, so try to avoid that, and feeding her too many nutes will make her limp and Dopey. Towards the end of the flowering stage Snow White will be loaded, and I do mean absolutely loaded, with dense, sticky buds that will turn her from an attractive plant into an absolute beauty queen. She might seem Bashful, but she actually loves the attention. The thick white hairs will cover the buds, making them appear even frostier than they already are; you might say they have buds as white as snow. The finished buds will be unbelievably resinous and sticky, and your final harvest should be massive, whether you're growing indoors or out!

Snow White buds smell absolutely glorious; fruity, sweet, and just like candyfloss. To preserve the sweet taste I like to smoke out of a nice clean bong, although that method makes this strain hit even harder. It's already a strain that will make you Sleepy, Happy and Dopey all at the same time, but a huge bong hit can also make you Coughy, Stoney and Is-he-passed-outy too!

Special Kannabia

Kannabia are one of my absolute favorite Spanish seed companies, and not just because they're heaps of fun or because one of the breeders has the same name as the best character from Spanish kid's TV show Pocoyo. No, I like Kannabia because they are incredibly good at what they do – and what they do is growing great marijuana. They have outdone themselves this time with this fantastic strain, which was created by breeding an Early Pearl x Skunk cross with an Afghani indica plant.

Despite its indica dominance, Special Kannabia plants tend to stretch a little more than normal and have larger intermodal spacing than you might be used to. The indica genetics are also less strong than other hybrids, meaning that these plants can take up to 3 months to be finished outdoors. It is resistant to extremes of temperature, however, and the Skunk phenotype is extremely bushy and delightful! These plants will get to 3 or 4 feet and yield 20 grams each indoors and 60 grams each outdoors. Harvest should be at around 8 to 9 weeks for optimal results!

**Kannabia Breeding
Team, Spain**
Indica-Dominant
Genetics: (Early Pearl x
Skunk) x Afghan
Potency: THC 18%
kannabia.es

These very heavy, hard nugs will show you why this strain is called "Special"; the balanced high is beautifully light but equally as effective, and the taste is just sublime. This Kannabia treat is certainly a Special strain that's more than worth a try!

Spiritual Punk

I think Spain's fantastic Samsara Seeds created this strain just for me. I may not have a mohawk or huge safety pins through my appendages anymore, but I still do listen to Crass and my John Cooper Clarke books are very well read. I always give the finger to the cops when driving by them in my friend's Prius and I do quite like that vegan restaurant round the corner from my house…. Am I a Spiritual Punk? I think so.

A cross between a real Mazar-I-Shariff plant and the ever-fantastic Northern Lights, the actual Spiritual Punk is very popular in Cali's medical clubs, which is a nice nod to the punk venue on Gilman Street – where I imagine it's very popular, too! As a 100% indica this plant is squat and bushy, with high resistance to disease and intensely dense buds. After a flowering time of 53 days, both indoor and outdoor growers can expect to harvest just under 500 grams per square yard of grow space.

The startling amount of resin on Spiritual Punk buds means that this strain is great for finger hash, which feels grassroots enough to be properly punk. The high will make you forget all your worries though, so to regain that real punk anger watch a few episodes of "My Super Sweet Sixteen" and feel nihilistic all over again!

Samsara Seeds, Spain

Indica-Dominant

Genetics: Northern Lights x Mazar

Potency: THC 18%

samsaraseeds.com

StarBerry

Holland's HortiLab Seed Company are very well known in their part of the world, not least because they make some absolutely fantastic Sour strains and are known for working with great genetics. This strain is a bit of a departure from the lines that they're most well known for, but it is certainly not a departure from the quality they always push forward. This strain is a cross between HortiLab's own StarBud female clone and a Blueberry male from DJ Short – definitely a star strain!

If you've ever grown DJ Short's famous Blueberry, then you'll find this strain a total doddle to cultivate. It's a small plant, as you would expect, although if you fail to keep your lights near the seedlings right from the moment they pop, you can experience a little more stretch than you will really want. To keep your lights at the correct distance, put your hand over the tips of the plants. If the light burns your hand, they are too close. Find the point where they just stop being too hot, and that is the perfect position for them. In the vegetative stage, this plant will exhibit some good branching and when

HortiLab Seed Company, Holland

Indica-Dominant

Genetics: StarBud x Blueberry

Potency: THC 19%

hortilab.nl

flowering begins, the bushy structure will fill out into an almost fluffy little plant, one that grows incredibly dense little nugs that are so hard they feel like big marbles. Because of this, this plant can be susceptible to mold in more humid environments, so outdoor growers in warm, wet countries should always check their plants thoroughly, and indoor growers should ensure that good ventilation is at the top of their to-do list. StarBerry can be grown in a hydro set up with great results, but will also be fairly happy in a soil grow with minimal nutrients. Be sure not to overwater, but instead keep a sharp eye on your babies and make sure they're getting just enough food. The flavor of the Blueberry father will come through in these perfect little buds, highlighted with purple and orange, so you'll want to do a very extensive flush for the 2 weeks before harvest to ensure you're getting the very best taste and aroma in your final product. StarBerry is a medium to high yielder, depending on the amount of light she gets, but indoor growers can expect a harvest that they'll be more than happy with!

As a heavy indica-dominant cross, StarBerry delivers a pretty strong body stone but it also has a nice little tickle of a head high that will keep you awake long enough to enjoy the effects! The long-lasting stone will have you sitting and "relaxing" for hours on end, debating everything from the meaning of life to whether *Machete* was as good as *Planet Terror*. And just FYI: it was better.

Sugar Loaf

Cannabis strains often have me feeling hungry and heading straight for the kitchen, but usually this is after I've smoked about 8 bowls and the munchies have got me firmly in their grasp. However, this hybrid strain from Spain's CannaBioGen had me feeling hungry before I'd ever picked up my pipe, and I wanted banana bread quite specifically; it was the most sugary loaf I could think of! The name, however, refers to the way that sugar used to be bought, back in Victorian times. Rather than the

CannaBioGen, Spain

Indica-Dominant

Genetics: Pakistani x

(Indian Manali x

Colombian)

cannabiogen.com

bags of the stuff that we load up on now, white sugar used to come pressed very heavily into cone shapes, and if you wanted to use any, you had to use specialized 'sugar nips' to hack off a bit and plop it into your tea. Once you've grown this plant, you can see why CannaBioGen thought the name was relevant; not only do these plants grow in that same conical shape, but they're also so covered in white crystals that you'd think they were made of sugar!

Sugar Loaf is a cross between a Pakistani indica plant and a hybrid of Indian Manali and Colombian genetics known as Capricho, so as you can imagine it is quite the exotic beauty when it grows! This strain is one that can be grown both indoors and out, and will grow with a fabulous vigor in either situation. Staking can be very helpful when growing Sugar Loaf, and the easiest way to do this is to stake early on and allow the plants to grow around them. In the later stages of flowering, the branches will also need to be tied to avoid them breaking. The vegetative period should be around 25 days, after which you should flip your plants into forced flowering for best results. The flowering period is around 60 days, which translates to a harvest around the beginning of October for outdoor growers. By this point, the sugary look of Sugar Loaf will be complete and you'll have to hold yourself back from licking the colas like a lollipop. I've tried it, and it's not a good idea.

The high calyx-to-leaf ratio of this plant makes trimming a doddle, and the good news is that the dried buds look just as amazing as they do on the plant. The smoke is as sweet as a chocolate drop and just as delightful, but it's the high that's the real cherry on top: a psychoactive high with just enough of a body stone to keep you from flying right out of your living room, down the street and far, far away!

The Beast

I don't know whether there's some sort of worldwise Disney resurgence going on these days, or whether the company just etched its movies into my subconsciousness so strongly when I was an infant that I see references in almost all places at all times, but there are a hell of a lot of strains lately that seem to me to have taken their titles from Mr. Walt's movies. What with Snow White also in this very book and this, a clear play on the story of Belle and her dopey father, I feel like I might as well call this book the World's Essential Guide to Cannabis Strains Named After Movies Made By A Potentially Anti-Semitic Animator. I won't though. The similarities between this strain and the prince-turned-beast can't be ignored, though; no one knows its parents, it's ridiculously strong, and when it's fully matured its almost totally covered in orange-brown hairs. I wouldn't be surprised if I found someone's French dad cowering in a basement somewhere in the North of Seeds grow facility — although it should be said that they're lovely guys!

North of Seeds, Spain

Indica-Dominant

Potency: THC 11-17%

northofseeds.com

Just like Disney's prince, when it's time for this plant to become The Beast it will grow almost before your very eyes. The hybrid vigor means that it will shoot up quickly, necessitating an almost daily raising of the lights in your grow room if you don't want the plants to burn their tips. The structure grows strong enough to withstand a hurricane, with extremely strong stems and thick, deep green leaves that are almost as wide as they are long. It does, however, have one Achilles heel; extreme humidity, both indoors and out, can foster the growth of mold and bud rot, so be sure to keep ventilation up, humidity down, and check often for mold on the tight little nugs. It takes 60 days for this strain to fully mature, which, if you're growing outdoors, translates to a harvest date of October 10th or just before. Indoor growers will harvest something in the region of 350 to 500 grams per square meter or grow space, while those lucky enough to grow this strain outdoors can expect to yield that amount from one single plant.

When you smoke up some buds of the Beast, you'll feel like you, too, are breaking out of your human shell and turning into a greater animal. Once the floral taste and smoke clears away, your skin will tingle, your muscles will tighten and you might even see your clothes begin to tear at the seams. Don't worry though, you'll chill out before you start to roar and instead, this heavy stone will turn you into a happy little puppy rolling over on its back to get a nice little belly rub.

The Hog

Holland's TH Seeds do great work with some wicked genetics, creating strains that even the most cynical of growers love to grow and the most hardened of tokers love to smoke. The Hog is a Hindu Kush x Afghani strain originally from Tennessee, which makes a nice change, that was taken over to Southern California about a decade ago and has been bred out by TH Seeds since then. It's a phenotype of Hogsbreath, which serious smokers love for its high and lingering effect.

This is a TH Seeds' quintessential indica strain, growing never higher than 3.5 feet tall and giving a great yield of around 450 grams per square meter of grow space. A SOG set up will give you the maximum possible yield from The Hog, especially when clones are flowered at around 4 inches and the density of the plants is around 4 per square foot. This is an easy strain to grow, though you need to keep humidity levels at around 45% at all times and keep an eye out for bud rot.

I think the Hog is so called because it is super stinky, so if you love funky-smelling strains and you're a Cheese fiend, you'll go mad over this one. However, it also hits as strongly as it reeks, and gives an extremely heavy, lethargic, narcotic couch-locker stone that hardcore tokers love but that might wipe rookie smokers right out!

TH Seeds, Holland

Indica-Dominant

Genetics: Hindu Kush x Afghani

Potency: THC 22%

thseeds.com

Cannabis Indica The Essential Guide to the World's Finest Marijuana Strains, Volume 2

168

The Purps

Canada's BC Bud Depot have got their hands on a real winner, here. The Purps is a strain of legend. A fantastic, stable, inbred line of the killer Mendo Purps that the breeders got as a gift at the 2004 Cannabis Cup. Having worked on this for two straight years before releasing it, BC Bud Depot now consider it to be one of their best strains; and given the quality of their catalogue, that's saying a lot.

If you veg the Purps for just 4 weeks, you can expect your plant to stay under 3 feet but branch out like Starbucks: somewhat excessively. This is a hardy plant that can adapt to almost any grow situation, but as The Purps has such a phenomenal flavor, an organic soil grow is probably the best way to go. Outdoor growers can expect to harvest in the middle of October.

The buds smell both Skunky and grape-like, and they look sexier than Sophia Loren smoking a blunt and pouring a beer. Harvesting your crop before the stated 7-8 week flowering time will ensure a slightly more heady high, though you can't really escape the couchlock that The Purps is going to bring. You can, though, keep this to a minimum and get yourself an intense heady high that's clear as a freshly cleaned window and as enjoyable as a night with the aforementioned Ms. Loren.

BC Bud Depot, Canada

Indica-Dominant

Genetics: Mendo Purps IBL

Potency: THC 20%

bcbuddepot.com

Thunderbud

I think if I was to go into professional wrestling, I would name myself after this strain. Thunderbud's gimmick would be to lift his legs like a sumo wrestler and bring them down to huge claps of thunder from the sound system. Thunderbud would also celebrate his many wins by getting mad high on Holy Smoke Seeds' Purple Urkel x Pineapple Funk cross whilst sitting on his opponent. I'm not sure if the WWE would really like it but I'd be every stoner's favorite wrestler!

In order to grow just like my Thunderbud namesake I'd have to get big real quick, have huge, strong arms and finish up with this image overhaul in just 9 weeks from the beginning. I would be quite tall but mostly wide, as Thunderbud is only slightly indica-dominant, but mostly I'd be chunky and dense, like the wicked purple nugs that populate Thunderbud plants towards the end of flowering. I'd also be pretty gorgeous to look at, but of course I'd have to cover that with manliness; no one wants a pretty wrestler.

The best thing about being Thunderbud, however, will be the sweet, fruity smoke that I get to enjoy when my opponent is eating the canvas and I'm chillin' with a bowl of my namesake. I'll be feelin' that nice balanced high, getting a lot of heady confidence and, most of all, relaxing into the knowledge that it's good to be Thunderbud.

Holy Smoke Seeds, UK
Indica-Dominant
Genetics: Purple Urkel x Pineapple Funk
Potency: THC 19%
puresativa.com

Cannabis Indica The Essential Guide to the World's Finest Marijuana Strains, Volume 2

Tingo Sour Kush

I know, I know. You think you've seen all the Sour Kush strains; you think you've smoked them all. Well, it's a good job that the USA's tissue culture experts BillBerry Farms are here to offer you a new and more interesting take on the Sour line than you're used to! By crossing NY Sour Diesel with OG Kush and MK Ultra back in 2010, these guys have not only brought together 3 of my all-time favorite strains, they've opened up a whole new world of Sour weed.

Though this strain can be grown indoors or outdoors, the breeder recommends that indoor growers who prefer a SOG set up should cut the center apex to encourage the plant to bush out. The breeder also states that, when cloning, you will need to give the babies extra attention and a lot of TLC. These plants hog the light so be sure to prevent them from overgrowing your other strains, and if you want to keep your plants 3 or 4 feet high instead of 9, keep the vegetative stage to a minimum.

The bright green Tingo Sour Kush nugs will taste of citrus fruit and oil, and will bring on a creeping kidnapper of a body high. You'll be sitting there chatting then, out of nowhere, this huge body buzz will puts its hand over your mouth and drag you away for a few hours. Don't worry; it will all be OK in the end!

BillBerry Farms, USA

Indica-Dominant

Genetics: MK Ultra x NY Sour Diesel x OG Kush

Potency: THC 19%

billberryfarmstissueculture.com

Top 69

I'll refrain from making the obvious jokes here. In fact, they're all pretty obvious so I'll refrain from making any jokes at all, save to say that the name of this strain definitely made me smile. I'm used to that when dealing with plants from Spain's Advanced Seeds, though, as they are well known for having some fantastic breeding stock comprising the best genetics you could hope to get your grubby little hands on. This strain takes Northern Lights as its base, but as ever, Advanced Seeds aren't happy with just pumping out another Northern Lights cross. No, for Top 69 they've gone even further and crossed that plant with a ruderalis variety to create an auto-flowering Northern Lights hybrid. Yep, you read that right.

As the Northern Lights hybrid parent of this strain leaned more towards the indica side, Top 69 is an indica-dominant cross and therefore is one that will be more than happy in your indoor grow room. In 3-gallon pots, plants will grow to around 3 feet tall, while outdoors they can get to 4 feet and slightly beyond, though the healthy dose of ruderalis genetics will always keep them fairly squat. These plants exhibit extensive branching, making them more than suitable for both SOG and ScrOG grow styles – and, in fact, this can be a great plant to try those styles with for the first time, as you don't need to worry about changing the light schedule and so can focus more on training the plants. Outdoor growers will find that this is a hardy plant, as the ruderalis genetics were originally found in very cold, super harsh climates. Even as their offspring, modern auto-flowering plants still preserve that tendency towards strength and resilience, which makes outdoor ruderalis grows incredibly hardy. The best time for growing Top 69, however, in the Northern Hemisphere, is still between April and November, though Top 69 will survive the colder snaps that some growers might experience towards the end of that period. Indoor production can reach up to 450 grams per square yard of grow room, while outdoors, this can be even higher. The plant will be finished in just 90 days from seed, meaning that even with only one grow set up, indoor growers can easily get 4 crops a year from Top 69.

Advanced Seeds, Spain

Indica-Dominant

Genetics: Northern Lights Hybrid x Ruderalis

Potency: THC 14%

advancedseeds.com

The breeders recommend this strain for relaxation and meditation, although I reckon that wanting to get a buzz on while watching reruns of "The Office" is just as valuable an experience when smoking Top 69. Expect a very sedative type of effect, as good for pain relief and inducing sleep as it is for bringing on the ever-famous munchies. Mine's a three-cheese pizza.

Tsi Fly

The Europe-based Mosca Seeds company hasn't been around all that long, but they have made enough impact on the breeding scene for you to think they've been in business since before you were born. Their Tsi Fly strain is one of the best from their collection, in my opinion, and not just because it beings together the genetic powerhouses of C4 and C99. The C4 female was convinced to go on a blind date with the C99 male, and as soon as these kids set eyes on each other, sparks flew; the breeders couldn't keep them off each other and soon a little Tsi Fly offspring came forth. The Mosca breeders have backcrossed this little guy to stabilize it and bring out its most desirable qualities, meaning that your crop will be as uniform as it will be beautiful!

You can't mistake a properly working grow room full of Tsi Fly: a glorious sea of 3 foot plants, all wide, deep green leaves and fat colas, all happily swaying gently in the breeze of the ventilation and looking so juicy that it's hard not to chew on a bud right there and then. Tsi Fly forms long colas that look like a sea of fat arms at a rock concert – the only difference being that these arms hold killer nugs rather than lighters, and the plants are wearing tshirts that state the band they're going to see on them. These plants will be fully finished after 60 days of flowering, and they won't stretch much at any stage of growth, so

Mosca Seeds, Europe

Indica-Dominant

Genetics: C4 x C99

Potency: THC 18%

seedsman.com

they make a great choice for the indoor grower. Just be aware that you might have to pump AC/DC and Springsteen in to their grow room to keep them super happy and convince them to produce the largest amount of bud possible. In order to preserve the absolutely killer taste of this strain, it's best to go with an organic grow or to flush with molasses in the final two weeks of flowering. Make sure you get any chemicals out! If you get growing conditions just right, your Tsi Fly harvest will be super heavy, with big tight nugs and dense colas.

Unusually, Tsi Fly buds taste very strongly of apricot, which is a nice surprise the first time you take in a full bong hit and don't know what's coming! This flavor took me right back to my Grandma's kitchen, when I was a chubby little kid eating apricot jam straight from the jar and getting it all over my fat face. The high is just as hectic as the taste; a serious double knock out punch that is like crashing your car into a giant pillow at high speed. Don't try to get up and don't try to make sense. Just enjoy the sit down stone and let it take you into sleep!

Vanilluna

If you haven't smoked DJ Short's game-changing Blueberry, than your career as a pot smoker has yet to reach its peak. If you have had the pleasure of puffing on a pipe of Blueberry, don't worry – you've still got a whole world of amazing Blue offspring to explore, too. Vanilluna is one of these, having been created from an Original Blueberry male and a Blueberry Sativa female. It's also known as Vanilla Moon, which makes me want to suck on the Earth's only satellite like a lollipop.

As a quasi-hybrid, Vanilluna grows to a medium height but in an indica growth pattern. 15% of Vanilluna plants will be varied in their growth, while the vast majority will give uniform plants. The flowering time of all types is between 55 and 60 days, after the buds have swollen to their largest size and the trichomes are absolutely gleaming. The breeders recommend giving these plants an extended vegetative period with early topping to increase the yield, although they also grow well untopped in a SOG system.

You'll understand why some call this strain Vanilla Moon when you're transported to a dreamy, chilled out planet of your own making after smoking a bowl or two. While your body is feeling fluffy your mind will be calm and clear, leaving you more relaxed than a fat old cat sitting in the sun and getting its belly rubbed. Pure bliss.

DJ Short Seeds, Canada

Indica-Dominant

Genetics: Blueberry Sativa x Original Blueberry

Potency: THC 17%

legendsseeds.com

greatcanadianseeds.com

Viuda Blanca

Spain's Pitt Bully Seeds are a great little company sending out some fantastic strains around Europe and beyond. Viuda Blanca, as any fans of mid-90s Colombian *telenovelas* will already know, is Spanish for White Widow – one of the most famous hybrid strains that has ever been released. This Spanish White Widow, however, is a little different to the one that many North American tokers may know and love. It still contains a mix of Brazilian Manga Rosa and a South Indian plant, but with a delightful Spanish flair. This makes for a very exotic cross, and one that is only marginally indica-dominant.

As with all more balanced hybrids, Viuda Blanca can grow taller than pure indica strains, topping out at up to 6 feet tall, although you can ensure that the plants don't grow beyond your grow room by cutting down on their vegetative stage and keeping them in smaller pots. Indoor plants will rarely grow beyond 3 feet in height. These plants are very adaptive to whatever situation you put them in and cherish the thrill that an outdoor guerrilla grow throws at them. Indoors, they can be easily grown in 2-gallon pots but they will need special attention when it comes to watering; make sure you don't overfeed but do make sure they've got enough water to thrive at all times.

Pitt Bully Seeds, Spain

Indica-Dominant

Genetics: Brazilian Manga Rosa x South Indian

Potency: THC 18-21%

pittbully.com

laabuelaverde.com

Outdoor growers can expect to harvest around 500 grams, while indoor growers should expect something in the region of 400 grams per square yard of grow space. Outdoor growers in the Northern Hemisphere should plant in April and harvest in September, while Southern growers should plant in October and harvest in March. The flowering time of this strain sits at 56 days, which, incidentally, is about as long as that Colombian *telenovela* feels like it goes on for.

With such a marginal prevalence of indica genetics over sativa, you would expect Viuda Blanca to have a particularly balanced high with the potential to sway one way or the other, depending on the smoker and the setting – and you'd be completely right. This is a chameleon of a stone, meaning that it will take on the properties of its background and setting and fit right in. If you're sailing through life on a natural high, then this will give you a step up and keep your mind going at full tilt. If you're feeling that you need to slow down, however, this strain can give you a relaxing head and body stone that seriously chills you out. Much like the Colombian *telenovela* subject that shares its name, Viuda Blanca will come in to your life, run riot, then be out of it again before you know it – so make sure you enjoy it while you have it! Maria!

Warlock

Originally produced by Magus Genetics and now being put out by the fantastic Serious Seeds, Warlock is, as you'd expect it to be, a solid and dependable strain that can pack a serious punch if you get on the wrong side of it! As an indica-dominant cross between Skunk #1 and an Afghani indica that was first released in the early 90s, this strain also has Mexican and Columbian heritage so is a very interesting strain to both grow and smoke!

Growers will love Warlock due to its lack of leaves and its huge density of flowers, even on smaller plants. This makes trimming an absolute dream, and you feel like Edward Scissorhands when after just a few seconds of chopping the nugs look good enough to eat! After a flowering time of 60 days you can expect to harvest up to 500 grams of awesome Warlock bud per square meter of grow space.

The word "warlock" comes from the Old Norse for "caller of spirits", and the sativa-like high of this strain certainly makes you feel that the spirits have been called right to you! With more of a head high than a body stone, this is a very active high, but don't be toking this before a marathon, heading out for a big grocery shop or in fact anything too taxing, as it does still numb your appendages out a fair bit!

Developed by Magus Genetics; now produced by Serious Seeds, Holland
Indica-Dominant
Genetics: Skunk/Afghani x Afghani
Potency: THC 20-23%
seriousseeds.com

Cannabis Indica The Essential Guide to the World's Finest Marijuana Strains, Volume 2

184

Westside

It's obvious to pretty much everyone in the European breeding scene that Holland's All Star Genetics have got some serious experience under their belts. They've been growing since the early 90s, and such fantastic strains as Westside illustrate that all this work has not been wasted! This Afghani x Northern Lights cross capitalizes on the great Northern Lights effect, whilst making this cross more weighted towards the indica influence and, therefore, much easier to grow.

This plant is a great indoor strain, as it grows only to 4 or 5 feet but yields a huge amount of great bud. It is also one of ASG's fastest strains, finishing fully between 8 and 9 weeks. If you're partial to outdoor growing then Westside will do fine there too, although watch out for mold in more humid climates. No matter where you grow this strain you can expect a killer harvest of around 450 grams per square meter of grow space, although you'd be forgiven for thinking that each bud weighs 450 grams itself, given the crazy density of these gorgeous nugs!

ASG Seeds, Holland

Indica-Dominant

Genetics: Afghani x Northern Lights

Potency: THC 18%

asgseeds.com

You can't get much more gorgeously indica than this type of strain; the subtle taste gives way to a totally unsubtle brick wall of a body stone that will pin you like Bret "The Hitman" Hart and lay you down like cheap laminate flooring. It's the best there is.

White Afghan

Philosopher Seeds are a cool company working out of Spain, where presumably they read the works of Plato, Goethe and Sartre when they're not breeding cannabis plants and getting mad high. Their White Afghan comprises Afghani and White Widow genetics, making it a fairly balanced hybrid with just a slight indica dominance.

These plants are very dense and stay very small, and so they work extremely well in a SOG operation. The breeders also comment that growing White Afghan at a density of 25 plants per square meter of grow space and using 3.5 liter pots is a fantastic way to really get the best out of this strain. If you prefer to grow with less density in your grow room, then topping the main cola might be preferred. This is an easy plant to look after, even for new and inexperienced growers, and should be ready for harvest in 55 days, or at the end of September in a Northern Hemisphere outdoor grow. Outdoor growers will get a yield of 450 grams per plant, whereas indoor growers can expect 350 grams per square yard of grow room.

Philosopher Seeds, Spain
Indica-Dominant
Genetics: Afghani x White Widow
Potency: THC 14-16%
philosopherseeds.com

This is the closest weed has ever come to smelling like a bunch of fresh-cut flowers, and the smoke is only slightly less wholesome-tasting. The high, too, is pretty clean cut: very clear, enjoyable head and body high that's great for a daytime toke!

Cannabis Indica The Essential Guide to the World's Finest Marijuana Strains, Volume 2

White Dwarf

Before now, I didn't realize that Spain's Buddha Seeds were amateur astrologists. Now I realize that they must be, to give this strain such a clever name. In astrology terms, a white dwarf —also known as a degenerate dwarf, which is a bit of a racial diss, if you ask me! – is what almost all the stars in our galaxy will eventually become, as they are not large or heavy enough to become neutron stars. In the simplest terms, a white dwarf is an incredibly dense small star, and amazingly enough this is also a perfect description of Buddha Seeds' Lowryder / White Widow cross. Was this just a cool fluke, or do the breeders at Buddha Seeds search the skies nightly for inspirations for their fantastic original strains? I guess we'll never know.

The Lowrdyer parentage of this strain makes it an autoflowering variety, so it needs no change of light cycle to flip into flowering; instead it just marches right into the final growth stage when it is good and ready! This is just another trait that makes White Dwarf such a 'star', but it's not the only one. White Dwarf, as the name suggests, is as small as it is dense, and is a great yielder for one that takes up such little space. In fact, for hobby growers who don't have much room, you'll be hard pressed to find a more suitable strain. It hardly needs any room, time or care, and you'll need to put more effort into actually killing the thing than you will need to put in to keep it alive! The most effort will be expended in germinating the seeds, which are made for harsh winters so don't pop as easily as some others. White Dwarf crops will be fully mature and ready for harvest after 8 weeks, regardless of the light cycles, so it doesn't matter if you grow it inside or outdoors; 8 weeks is all it will ever need. It is also quite the looker; the buds are totally white, and to my delight especially, look like miniature Christmas trees that have been dusted with the first snows of winter. I might be getting a tad overly romantic here, but it's difficult not to when your plants are so goof looking!

Buddha Seeds, Spain
Auto-Flowering Indica-Dominant
Genetics: Lowryder x White Widow
Potency: THC 15%
buddhaseedbank.com

Like the heat of a white dwarf just after it's formed, the high of this strain will feel explosive at first, but will gradually radiate away down the rest of your body and will calm down from there. Also like a white dwarf, the high is a lingerer, and will continue to be there for what feels like several million light years. If this strain doesn't have you buying a telescope and staring at the skies while you're high as a far sun, I don't know what will. A star in every sense of the word!

White Siberian

Dinafem have spent the last few years absolutely killing it in their native Spain and beyond. Their strains always hit the mark with their genetics and their fantastic good looks. White Siberian is a mix of White Widow and AK-47 genetics, hence the nod to Russia in its name, and with such quality parental genetics this little strain has a lot to live up to!

Thankfully, White Siberian more than delivers on the promise of its parents; finishing in 60 days, and mid October outdoors, this plant can grow up to 8 feet outside thanks to its strong sativa influence along with the indica prevalence. The wide, deep green leaves are a delight for indica lovers and it grows at a moderate speed, making it asy to manage. It's also an extremely hardy plant, resistant to colder temperatures out in the wild and absolutely covered in resin when the time for harvest comes around!

Your finished White Siberian buds will be anything but white, with hues of green and flourishes of orange making the nugs look like candy wrappers. The flavor is like pineapple – fruity but with a harsh tang – and the effect has a good dose of sativa psychoactivity all wrapped up in a great and long-lasting indica body buzz. It's the best of both worlds, a perfect hybrid of two great strains and a treat for all!

Dinafem Seeds, Spain

Indica-Dominant

Genetics: White Widow x AK-47

Potency: THC 12-19%

dinafem.org

Wild Zombie

I should probably state right now that I am a huge fan of Rob Zombie, George A. Romero, "Dead Set" (Google it) and "The Walking Dead," so I was always going to love this strain from America's Bortnick Farms. However, even those who don't enjoy their dead undead will love Wild Zombie for the quality of its genetics, coming as they do from White Widow, Kush, Purple Kush and Big Blue.

Like its namesakes, it is almost impossible to kill this strain. It can handle very excessive conditions, and will continue to thrive even when you think it must be dead and gone. Clones of Wild Zombie will be just as difficult to get rid of, and once they mature these kids can grow to 7 feet or more indoors. The only way to stop Wild Zombie is to chop off the head – and the arms, and the rest of it entirely, dry the buds and get mad high. This should only be done after 56 days, otherwise you might anger the rest of the crop, and who knows what might happen then?

Wild Zombie will trick you with its incredibly sweet smell and orangey taste, then when you're not looking…BAM! You'll feel it bite right in, then your body will slowly wind down and stop. Your body won't be yours to control, and the only sounds coming from you will be muffled groans. Sounds like a great night to me!

Bortnick Farms, USA
Indica-Dominant
Genetics: (White Widow x Kush) x Big Blue x Purple Kush
Potency: 20%

PHOTOS BY MARIJUANA MAX

Zei

Switzerland's Tiki Seedbank may not be as well known as Greenhouse or Sensi Seeds, but the work they're doing in their native Europe is more than worthy of world-wide respect. The head breeder at Tiki discovered hemp cultivation back in the early 80s, when he first began growing outdoors with seeds from Thailand. Later that decade he brought seeds back from Mexico, then in the next few decades he went around the world collecting fantastic seeds from such places as Pakistan, Colombia, Ghana, Morocco and Nepal. This endeavor was never intended to end with a seed company, but rather to end up with the plants that the breeder himself considered perfect – but the reaction of his friends to the resulting plants meant that the idea for the Tiki Seedbank was planted (if you'll pardon the pun) and never went away. This strain combines two of his best plants, Mazar and his own Shulam strain, to create a new Swiss classic that should be smoked around the world!

Zei is a great choice for indoor growers, as its heavy indica dominance means that it stays short, squat and incredibly bushy throughout its life cycle. With a maximum height of 3 feet, even a hobby grower with only a college dorm to grow in can grow enough Zei weed to keep himself high as a kite for the whole semester. These plants will grow with a centralized cola and a very compact, very strong structure; a herd of cows could stomp through your grow room and your Zei plants would probably still be standing. I don't recommend trying this, though. The structure of your plant will tighten up during its vegetative growth period and it won't tend to stretch during this time at all. The breeder tells us that this strain is great for taking clones that are meant to be flowered immediately – a trick that will keep your plants even smaller and enhance the use of your grow space even more. Both indoor and outdoor growers can expect a harvest that's beyond the usual, and all with a flowering period of 55 days. Outdoor growers should be ready to harvest around the end of October, if growing in the Northern Hemisphere.

Tiki Seedbank, Switzerland
Indica-Dominant
Genetics: Mazar x Shulam
Potency: THC 18-20%
tikiseedbank.com

This is a great indica-dominant strain with an almost perfect indica effect, making it great for patients with chronic body pain. The effect is a very relaxed one, with a stone that rolls in slowly and sets up camp for as long as you want it to. It's perfect pot for the end of a party or for a lazy Sunday in summer when you want to do nothing more than chill in the sun with a cider and a corndog.

Zensation

Holland's Ministry of Cannabis might not be an official governmental department, but they certainly do act like one. They only give away their breeding secrets on a strict need-to-know basis, and as most of us don't need to know, we're a little out of luck. They can tell us, however, that their fabulous Zensation brings together genetics from an indica hybrid and a strain from the White family, which in itself is enough to make most tokers more than a little intrigued.

The indica influence shows itself in the Zensation growth pattern, as it only gets to 3.5 feet tall and finishes fully in between 8 and 9 weeks. The breeders recommend topping your Zensation crop to encourage the best growth, but beware not to fertilize too much or the plants will not be pleased. An outdoor Zensation plant can yield up to 400 grams.

Zensation is extremely strong and very long lasting, so settle in for a good session rather than smoking this as a wake 'n bake. Interestingly, this strain comes highly recommended as one that's great to toke before you "get down to business," if you know what I mean. It might not be an herbal alternative to Viagra but it will get your blow flowing and your mind running riot – so light the candles and put on some Barry White!

Ministry of Cannabis, Holland

Indica-Dominant

Genetics: Indica Hybrid x White Strain

Potency: THC 20-24%

ministryofcannabis.com

Zindica

The USA's Bumboklot Seeds (and if you don't know what Bumboklot is in Jamaican slang, I don't want to tell you) was founded by the great breeder Bumboklot, a man who has over 35 years of growing experience behind him and isn't afraid to show it! This strain is a blend of Northern Lights, G-13, AK-47 and Jamaican Kingsbreed genetics, which is about the equivalent of getting Angelina Jolie pregnant by Johnny Depp, Will Smith and Brad Pitt all at the same time and then putting that kid into acting school: it's always going to be a winner.

With such a star on your hands you don't want to treat her with anything but respect, so preserve Zindica's best traits by growing in a high-quality soil mix with as few nutrients as you can manage — she can handle herself pretty well without the help of enhancements, but a little extra feeding won't hurt. The breeder recommends a 10-gallon container, which seems a little harsh on such a princess, if you ask me!

It's not just Zindica's looks that will make you, and the rest of the world, fall in love with her; she packs an amazing stone that's balanced and strong without being overbearing. She tastes like grapefruit and smokes like a dream, and she's a hell of a lot of fun to be around — in fact, she might just be the perfect woman!

Bumboklot Seeds, USA
Indica-Dominant
Genetics: NL x G-13 x
AK-47 x Jamaican
Kingsbreed
Potency: THC 19%
holistichealthed.com

Index

Index

Index

Index